D0775666

Winter Trails: Vermont and New Hampshire

"An excellent guide! Keep *Winter Trails* in your backpack. Marty Basch is your 'personal guide' to the trails of Vermont and New Hampshire. Complete, concise, and elegantly descriptive!"

—Jim Radtke, editor-in-chief, *The Snowshoer* magazine

"*Winter Trails: Vermont and New Hampshire* is a user-friendly guide that will lead cross-country skiers and snowshoers to some of the best snow and most scenic landscapes in the East."

—David Goodman, contributing editor, *Ski, Powder,* and *Backcountry* magazines

"You'll appreciate this guide's at-a-glance practicality and its engaging depictions of each trip's unique features. . . . By paying snowshoeing its due, this guide helps a new segment of outdoor adventurers enjoy the winter's glory."

—Jason Brady, publisher, *Northeast Adventure Magazine*

Help Us Keep This Guide Up to Date

Every effort has been made by the author and editors to make this guide as accurate and useful as possible. However, many things can change after a guide is published—new products and information become available, regulations change, techniques evolve, etc.

We would love to hear from you concerning your experiences with this guide and how you feel it could be improved and be kept up to date. While we may not be able to respond to all comments and suggestions, we'll take them to heart and we'll make certain to share them with the author. Please send your comments and suggestions to the following address:

The Globe Pequot Press
Reader Response/Editorial Department
P.O. Box 833
Old Saybrook, CT 06475

Or you may e-mail us at:
editorial@globe-pequot.com

Thanks for your input, and happy travels!

WINTER TRAILS™ SERIES

winter trails™

Vermont & New Hampshire

The Best Cross-Country Ski & Snowshoe Trails

by
MARTY BASCH

The Globe Pequot Press

OLD SAYBROOK, CONNECTICUT

The Globe Pequot Press and the author assume no liability for
accidents happening to, or injuries sustained by, readers who engage
in the activities described in this book.

Copyright © 1999 by Marty Basch

All rights reserved. No part of this book may be reproduced or transmitted in
any form by any means, electronic or mechanical, including photocopying and
recording, or by any information storage and retrieval system, except as
expressly permitted by the 1976 Copyright Act or by the publisher. Requests
for permission should be made in writing to The Globe Pequot Press, P.O. Box
833, Old Saybrook, Connecticut 06475.

Winter Trails is a trademark of The Globe Pequot Press.

Cover photographs: Dennis Welsh/Adventure Photo & Film; inset photo ©
Gary Brattnacher and Adventure Photo & Film
Cover and interior design: Nancy Freeborn
Trail Maps created by Equator Graphics © The Globe Pequot Press
State maps: Lisa Reneson
Photo credits: pages xvii, 47, by Jan Duprey; all other photos by Marty Basch.

Library of Congress Cataloging-in-Publication Data

Basch, Marty.
      Winter trails of Vermont and New Hampshire : the best cross-country
  ski & snowshoe trails / by Marty Basch. — 1st ed.
          p.   cm. — (Winter trails series)
      Includes bibliographical references (p.   ).
      ISBN 0-7627-0305-9
      1. Cross-country skiing—Vermont—Guidebooks.   2. Cross-country
  skiing—New Hampshire—Guidebooks.   3. Cross-country ski trails—
  Vermont—Guidebooks.   4. Cross-country ski trails—New Hampshire—
  Guidebooks.   5. Vermont—Guidebooks.   6. New Hampshire—Guidebooks.
      I. Title.   II. Series.
      GV854.5.V5B37   1998
      917.4204'43—dc21   98-36049
                                                                    CIP

Manufactured in the United States of America
First Edition/First Printing

To Jan Duprey,

Sunshine on a winter's day.

Vermont

78
89
111 114
2
5 105 114
5 100
89
105
5
3 15 2
Essex 100
Junction Stowe 5
Underhill 6 Craftsbury
Center 15 Common
89
7 Marshfield
9 2
Huntington 8 Waterbury
2 Montpelier 1
93
302
17
12 5
7
Ripton 100 14 110
89
11
Goshen
7 100 107
5
Woodstock
4 12
Killington 4 10
100 106 91
103
7
14
Landgrove 5
13
Rupert
7A 100
16
18
Jamaica Grafton
15 Stratton 30 91
7A
100
9 Wilmington
7 17
5

Contents

New Hampshire

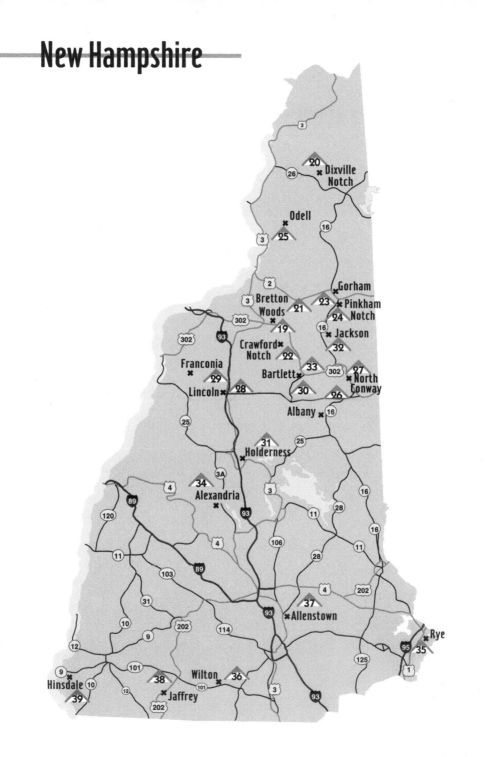

3

20 × Dixville
Notch

26

Odell
×

3 25

2

Gorham
×

3 Bretton
Woods 21 23 × Pinkham
302 24 Notch

16
302 19

302 16 × Jackson
93 Crawford× 32
Notch 22

Franconia 33 27
× Bartlett 302 × North
29 30 26 Conway

Lincoln× 28

Albany × 16

25

31 25
Holderness ×

3A

4 34 3
Alexandria
× 16
93
89 28
120
11 16

4
106 11
11 × 89
103
28

4 202

31 37
× Allenstown

10 93
9 202 114
Rye
12 ×
125 95 35

9 101
Hinsdale 10 38 Wilton 36 1
× ×
12 Jaffrey 101
39 × 93
202 3

new hampshire

Acknowledgments

Over the rivers and through the woods in winter can be an exhilarating experience. And it's nice to have company, either physically or in spirit. Thanks to the following people who were most helpful in either accompanying me or pointing the way during the research for this book: Jan Duprey; Steve and Brian Finch; Paula Brisco; Dan Spinella; Shelley Wolf; Alex Tait and David Swanson of Equator Graphics; David Nesbitt of The Balsams; Ben Wilcox at Bretton Woods; the Appalachian Mountain Club's Rob Burbank; Jackson Ski Touring's Thom Perkins; Kathleen Murphy at Tubbs Snowshoes; Roger Hill and Myra Foster at Stratton; Rolf Anderson and Mary Williams of the Green Mountain Club; John Rubright at Rikert's, Colin Lawson (thanks for the stuffed pretzels) at Grafton Ponds; Michael Walsh and Andrew Zboray of Monadnock State Park; Vermont state forester Gary Sawyer; Laurie Adams; Charlie Yerrick at Trapp's; Tony Clark at Blueberry Hill; Mike Miller at Mountain Meadows; Heidi White and Bill Altenburg at Phillips Brook Backcountry Recreation Area; John Wiggin at Woodstock; John Brodhead at Craftsbury Common; and the employees at the drug and alcohol rehabilitation center who let me use the phone to call AAA after I discovered that warning signs on certain snow-covered Vermont dirt roads are there for a reason.

Introduction

Welcome to winter!

Miles and miles of trails wind through the snow-encrusted forests, mountains, and valleys of Vermont and New Hampshire. Nature centers, state parks, national forests, community recreation areas, downhill and cross-country ski areas, open fields, and your own backyards all provide access to winter trails.

Trails that by summer take hikers to the summit of a 4,000-footer or meander gently around a pond reflecting the autumn sun become paths to ply for cross-country skiers and snowshoers.

Those who love winter know the silence of a trek in solitary woods. They see the beauty after a snowfall in a pine forest. They know the bugs are gone and there are fewer people. The cold doesn't bother them. Instead it becomes a challenge unto itself.

Those who love winter also know about the dangers that lurk around the bend. Changing weather, sudden squalls, flimsy ice, and more can turn a nice day into a survival test.

For those who prefer human-powered transportation, winter is a time for cross-country skiing and snowshoeing. Each mode of travel has its own benefits. If you can walk, you can snowshoe. If you can walk, you can cross-country ski, too, but it might take considerably more effort. Nonetheless, experiencing winter can be enjoyable.

Vermont and New Hampshire are home to a multitude of winter trails. The outings in this book cover trips in the Green Mountain National Forest in Vermont and the White Mountain National Forest of New Hampshire. There are also excursions through state parks, conservancy lands, and cross-country ski areas. Most of the outings do not have a fee, though trail passes are needed at the cross-country ski areas. In 1996 the White Mountain National Forest instituted a three-year pilot program that requires users to purchase a recreation pass when parking at trailheads within the forest boundaries.

Skiers and snowshoers aren't the only recreationalists using the winter trails. You will also encounter hikers and snowmobilers on certain outings. Trails that are used by snowmobilers are kept at an absolute minimum in this book.

Each outing is rated for difficulty, has driving directions to the trailhead and trail directions, offers suggestions for last minute groceries and a posttrip meal, comes with helpful phone numbers, and provides the distance of each journey. The trips can take a full day or just a couple of hours.

Whichever way you get around the trails of winter, stay sharp and enjoy.

Equipment

Technology marches on. If you are paying any attention to what you strap to your feet, you'll see that snowshoe and cross-country ski equipment has made a bit of a leap since its early users, like the Vikings or Eskimos, romped through the woods and across the tundra.

Don't fret. The old stuff still works. Those wooden ash snowshoes over the fireplace, in the attic, or on the wall of the garage will still do the trick. So will those three-pin skinny skis you bought at a yard sale on a whim a decade or so ago. Actually, if you tackle some of the trails in the White Mountains suggested in this book, be sure to stop in at Baldy's on the Kancamagus Highway and ask to see the snowshoe museum in the back. You'll see some excellent examples of what people used to use in the snow.

Wooden snowshoes with the basic bear-paw design are still being made, but the shape of the snowshoe has changed to become more streamlined. There is more choice as far as bindings go, and the snowshoe has become more light weight. Modern day snowshoes are also coming with affixed crampons, fingerlike plates that prevent slipping.

If you are new to snowshoeing and not sure if you are going to like it, the best bet is to rent a pair of snowshoes at a sporting goods store or cross-country ski center. Don't be afraid to pepper the staff with questions. That's what they are there for.

How do you choose the right snowshoe for you? There is a three-step process based on snow conditions, terrain, body weight, and price.

The first thing to do is figure out what kind of snowshoeing you plan to do. Most activity falls into either a recreational or mountaineering category. Recreational snowshoeing revolves around

A snowshoer prepares her gear to tackle Mount Tom in Woodstock, Vermont.

family outings, walking, running, hiking, aerobic cross-training, and day treks. These are the activities usually done on easy, broken trails. Mountaineering centers around wilderness excursions, overnight adventures, climbing approaches, and steep terrain. These outings are usually done in varying conditions from deep powder to unbroken trails to windswept snow.

Next, figure out your total body weight. That's not just how much you weigh, but the weight of the total package—body, clothing, and anticipated weight of backpacks.

The last step is to compare snowshoes. Based on how you expect to use them, take a look around the store. Ask about prices. Sample the various bindings to figure out which one will work best for you. Remember, the outdoors in winter will be a lot colder than a retail store. Make sure the equipment you buy is easy to use.

Some snowshoers use ski poles while on a trek. They are useful during ascents and descents. Lean on them if a tree isn't available.

Choosing the right cross-country ski equipment is a bit more complicated because you must purchase skis, boots, bindings, and poles. Basically, you can choose from waxable or waxless skis that are used for recreational or backcountry skiing. Of course, groups have subcategories that are based on weight, ability, style, and terrain. Nordic skiers also must decide if they want a ski for skating or the classical technique.

If you just want to get out and back on easy terrain at your local park or cross-country ski area, stick to the waxless skis. They perform well under most conditions, and you don't have to worry about waxing.

Racers and better skiers like waxable skis. They can get more glide out of the ski, which usually means a bit less work. But you must learn the right way to wax them, based on temperature and snow conditions.

As for the type of ski to get, as with snowshoeing, figure out what kind of skiing you want to do. Those skiers who like groomed and tracked trails stick to recreational skis, while those who prefer more untamed conditions gravitate to the wider, stronger-edged skis.

Proper Clothing

Wondering what to wear when heading outside to snowshoe or cross-country ski? Just remember one word—*layers*. Even though it could be downright cold outside, get ready to be quite warm while engaged in activity. You'll cool off quickly when you stop. To dress for comfort, choose lightweight and breathable underwear as a first layer. On top of that have an absorbent layer, like a sweater or fleece. The outside layer should be a wind-resistant shell.

The idea behind dressing this way is to better manage your body's temperature while snowshoeing or skiing. Layering gives you greater control than one thick layer of insulation, like a parka, does. By putting on and taking off layers, you act like a thermostat, regulating the body's temperature. As you exert more energy, your body will start to heat up. When that happens, remove a layer. Cold? Put layers back on.

The first layer is responsible for your skin. Perspiration is no fun in winter. That's why it's best to stay away from cotton and consider a layer that wicks away wetness from the skin and traps a blanket of dry, warm air. The middle layer has a couple of jobs. One is to encourage the perspiration to get on out of there. The other is to insulate by trapping warm air. Materials like fleece or wool are able to maintain that insulting quality even when wet.

The same principle applies to pants, although, in general, your legs don't need as much insulation as your upper body. Still, the layer next to your skin should be just like that next to the torso. On extremely cold, windy, or rainy days, a shell should be used on top of the insulating layer.

A hat is of primary importance. The head is a source of heat loss. Cover it to stay warm and dry. Take your hat off to cool down. Gloves and mittens are also part of the proper clothing arsenal. You should wear fleece, wool, or insulated gloves. A fleece glove with an overmitt is excellent on extreme weather days. The choice between glove or mittens is as personal as the choice of socks.

Dry and warm feet are happy feet. Happy feet are essential to an outdoor winter experience. Forget cotton. Fleece and wool are the mantra. Some people like two layers of socks, one thin and the other thick. It's your choice.

Cross-country skiers have a couple of choices for their boots. For the most part, low-cut boots are better for groomed trails. Higher boots that go above the ankle offer better support and are usually associated with deeper, ungroomed snow conditions.

Snowshoers and a cross-country skier share the trail on the grounds of the Trapp Family Lodge.

Waterproof hiking boots with decent ankle support should prove well suited for snowshoers. Plastic mountaineering boots can also be used for extended trips. For those casual outings, you can wear almost anything. But the idea is to stay warm and dry, so any rubber, insulated, or hiking boot will suffice.

A few accessories are helpful during an outdoor winter excursion. A neck warmer is an excellent choice. Not only will it keep your neck warm, it can also double as a goofy looking hat, wearable in the solitude of the woods. Your neck warmer can also triple as a headband if it is folded in half. A headband keeps ears warm on those sunny winter days called "spring." Gaiters are also a good idea. They keep the snow from getting in between your boots and socks.

Squinting can be minimized by using sunglasses. Extreme days call for goggles to protect eyes from the wind and cold. If vanity is a concern, always carry a baseball cap to ward off "hathead."

Consider a camera or binoculars for capturing those wonderful human and wildlife moments.

Safety

In winter trail conditions can vary drastically from day to day. Both the Appalachian Mountain Club and the Green Mountain Club agree that when using trails for winter travel, plan ahead. Winter in Vermont and New Hampshire can be unpredictable and severe. Changing weather, dropping temperatures, shorter days, and deep snow are all challenges you'll encounter while out on skis and snowshoes. Breaking trail can be an exhaustive experience. If an excursion takes you to higher elevations over open rock faces and above the treeline, snowshoes with crampons are necessary. It is imperative that you take extra warm clothing and a few safety items. Winter is rather harsh on mistakes. Though what you carry in a backpack or fanny pack is a personal choice, some suggested items include a guidebook, map, compass, insulated water bottles, high-energy foods, waterproof matches, flashlight with spare batteries (kept warm), rope, duct tape, toilet paper, and ski wax.

First-aid kits are also recommended. They can include items like pain relief medicine, adhesive bandages, gauze, ace bandages, and antiseptics.

Hypothermia and frostbite are dangerous threats in winter. Hypothermia, considered the leading cause for backcountry emergencies, occurs when the body's core temperature drops below normal. The most important impact of hypothermia is that it impairs judgment. Symptoms include shivering, disorientation, loss of coordination, and slurred speech. In order to prevent hypothermia, wear clothing that keeps you well insulated. Be sure to stay dry. Hydrate. Drink more than you think you need. Keep an eye on the weather. Be cognizant of the conditions of people you are traveling with.

Frostbite is the result of tissue being damaged by severe cold and wind. Pale skin and numbness are the two basic symptoms, though as the condition worsens, the affected area can freeze. Like hypothermia, frostbite can be prevented by wearing proper clothing that provides warmth and allows for flowing circulation. It is important to eat and hydrate well.

Before heading out, always plan ahead. Remember, there is safety in numbers. If you are inexperienced, don't head out alone. Take into consideration the abilities of those in your group, the weather, terrain, and hours of light left in the day. Many outdoor clubs, organizations, schools, and community centers offer first-aid and outside skill courses and workshops. Take one.

Above all, use common sense.

Navigation

Getting lost on a trail in winter is relatively easy. All you have to do is not pay attention and a pleasant day snowshoeing up the side of a 4,000-footer can turn into a race against daylight and disaster. Though beautiful, the whiteness of winter is also deceiving because it blankets landmarks that may be familiar to summer hikers and walkers. The soft and airy flakes can cover a stream where one misstep can plunge you into icy wetness. Stray just a few inches off the main trail and you may find yourself thigh-deep in a cold, hard, snowy trap.

In general it is easy to snowshoe or cross-country ski at a groomed, ski center, where a fee is charged. Maps are available before heading out, and trails are usually well signed with arrows pointing the way. Many centers have maps along the way, especially at junctions, that indicate where you are within the network. To alleviate any concerns, it is always best to question the frontline warrior behind the desk in the office for the latest information. This helpful person can even outline the route with a transparent marker to allay any fears. Cross-country ski networks are patrolled as well; experienced personnel look for skiers and shoers on the trails before the system shuts down for the day.

To avoid any confusion, always stick to the trail.

In the woods and forests, blazes are the key to successful navigation. Trees are marked at varying intervals with different colored paint. Follow the blazes and you are following the trails. Signs also mark the way. But in winter the snow can either cover or obscure a blaze. Severe storms can

Some winter trails offer cabins for an overnight stay.

throw blowdowns in the path, which can be confusing. And should you be on the Long Trail in Vermont, be particularly alert. The trail was not designed for winter use. It is blazed in white with markings four to five feet above the ground. During periods of soft light and deep snow, these can be hard to spot.

Of course following other people's tracks makes navigation easy. But if you are trailblazing in unfamiliar terrain, the task increases in difficulty. Always look for blazes. Consider trips that are out and back. That way, you can follow your tracks back.

Carry a map and a compass. Know how to use them.

Courtesy

The popularity of snowshoeing has boomed. With such popularity comes the responsibility of courtesy and etiquette for both the snow-shoer and skier. Snowshoeing in deep snow is fun, but many like the groomed, compacted trails at a cross-country ski area. There are some areas that forbid snowshoeing on the groomed trails, instead providing snowshoers with trails all their own. However, snowshoers and skiers do share many trails—both in fee areas and in the woods.

Give skiers the right of way. Skiers are generally going faster than snowshoers. Plus it's easier and quicker to get around on snowshoes.

Don't snowshoe on ski tracks. The beauty of the snowshoe is that it can virtually go anywhere. If you are snowshoeing on a skating lane, stay to the right. If possible stick to the edge of the trail and on the deeper snow. Skiing on tracks marred by snowshoe prints is nerve wracking.

Follow the rules. If you are at a ski center, stick to the rules. If in the woods, and a trail says for skiers only, abide by it.

Trail Classification

The outings in the "Winter Trails" series are based on a three-tier classification system—easiest, more difficult, most difficult. There aren't any hard-and-fast rules for determining the level of difficulty. In general an outing rated easiest is one that has flat and gentle terrain. It can be done in a couple of hours. A more difficult excursion has more rolling terrain. Better technique is needed to conquer the hills. The distance is a bit longer than on an easy trip. A most difficult outing has the most challenging terrain, requires advanced skill levels, and can be long and/or remote. Elevation can also play a factor.

Please note that a trail that might be easiest on snowshoes is not always easiest on skis. Heading down or up a particular section of a trail on snowshoes is a far different experience than on skis. Consider your outings accordingly.

Key to Icons

cross-country skiing trail

snowshoeing trail

skate skiing (skating) trail

The tracks of a cross-country skier make their way across Osmore Pond.

vermont

Osmore Pond Loop

Groton State Forest, Marshfield, Vermont

Type of trail:	
Also used by:	Hikers
Distance:	3.3 miles
Terrain:	Flat
Trail difficulty:	Easiest
Surface quality:	Ungroomed, but skier and snowshoe packed
Food and facilities:	Bring all you need on this loop, food and water not available. There are several outhouses along the way and three lean-to shelters for overnight accommodations. There is also a picnic area, and good eating at the P and H Truck Stop (802–429–2141) in Well's River.
Phone numbers:	For Vermont State Parks headquarters in Waterbury, (802) 241-3655.

Though only about a half hour's drive from places like the state capital of Montpelier and St. Johnsbury, Groton State Forest has a remote feel to it. The forest is used by hikers, naturalists, snowmobilers, snowshoers, and cross-country skiers, while supporting four-legged wildlife, such as black bear, moose, deer, mink, and beaver, as well.

There is room for every sort of creature in its 25,000 acres, making it the second-largest contiguous landholding by the state. The forest's history is linked to logging and the railroad. When the Montpelier to Wells River Railroad opened in 1873, it went through the forest. By the 1920s most of the timber was cut. Fire has also ravaged the area. One in 1903 put a new spin on the landscape, changing it from spruce, fir, and pine to red maple and birch.

The Civilian Conservation Corps came to the rescue in the 1930s, camping by the shores of Osmore Pond while planting pine and spruce.

A sign for Osmore Pond Loop points the way for the trail around the Vermont pond.

The rough topography and poor drainage in this forest is blamed on a glacier that crept through some 10,000 years ago, depositing gravel, sand, silt, and boulders.

The Osmore Pond Loop is a hiking trail that encircles the shores of the pond for about 2 miles. The path is clearly blazed in blue and has a few wet areas with narrow footbridges to cross. It is an outing made for both the family or those looking for an easy few hours out in the warming winter sun. The three lean-to shelters on the eastern side of the pond make the loop appealing for an overnight stay. The lean-tos each have an outhouse and fire pit, though no water is available. The picnic area on the western side of the pond offers an opportunity for al fresco dining by water's edge or under the roof of a shelter.

The trailhead, at the entrance to the New Discovery Campground, is well plowed. Park here by the tollgate and head straight on the campground road through the New Discovery Campground. It is on this section of your route that you might meet snowmobiles. Continuing on, the road comes to a junction (there's a portable toilet on the left and a bathhouse on the right). Straight ahead are large blue blazes. Head for them. This is the New Discovery Trail, and it will be the path for about 0.5 mile. The trail heads downhill, passing by a

Directions at a glance

0.0   Head straight down the campground road through the New Discovery Campground Lot B.

02.   There is a junction here. The New Discovery Trail, though not signed, is well marked with blue blazes. The trail begins straight and runs between the bathhouse on the right and site 39 on the left.

0.7   Junction with Osmore Pond Loop. Turn right on Osmore Pond Loop.

1.5   Junction with Little Deer Trail, which leaves right. Turn left toward the pond to continue on Osmore Pond Loop (Big Deer Mountain/Lake Groton/ Peacham Pond signs).

1.7   Bear left on Osmore Pond Loop at junction with Hosmer Brook, Big Deer Mountain, and Cold-water Brook Trails.

2.6   Turn left on New Discovery Trail and continue to trailhead.

spruce-fir stand, crossing another camp road, and then ending at a junction with the Osmore Pond Loop. The loop can be done in either direction, but we followed the posted arrow and turned right.

The Osmore Pond Loop hugs the shore and offers many a fine view of the neighboring hills and peaks. At a few sections the poor drainage is evident as narrow footbridges cross over boggy and marshy areas. It's not too long before you reach the picnic area. The sheltered picnic site is up on a small hill, while other tables are near the pond's edge.

From here, the trail winds along the shore, passing another boggy area that has narrow footbridges. At 0.6 mile from the picnic area the trail crosses under power lines and becomes bumpy but fun. Turn left at the junction with the Little Deer Trail. The Little Deer Trail heads right to the ridge atop the mountain. The Osmore Pond Trail turns left and skirts the southern edge of the pond. A wide bridge crosses the running waters of Hosmer Brook. After the bridge you'll spot the first of the three lean-tos, along with its outhouse.

There are a few wet spots on the eastern side too. A junction with the Hosmer Brook, Big Deer Mountain, and Coldwater Brook Trails is easily navigable.

The three lean-tos are spread out over the remainder of the loop and offer quiet places to rest and enjoy. The trail slices through the woods where giant marshmallows, really glacial boulders covered in snow, line the forest floor. New growth evergreens sprout up.

As the loop continues to the northern tip of the pond, it becomes much wetter, particularly its final stretch.

You'll experience déjà vu when you encounter the sign for the New Discovery Trail on the right. Turn right and head uphill, following the same path that took you to the pond. It's about 0.7 mile back to the car from here.

How to get There
From Montpelier or St. Johnsbury, travel on Route 2 to Route 232 south. The trailhead is on the left. From Well's River travel on Route 302 to Route 232 south. The trailhead is on the right. The signs in Groton State Forest are not up during winter. The New Discovery Campground, where this loop begins, is about a half mile north from the maintenance department on Route 232. The trailhead is marked by a white house and a plowed area with tollhouse.

Nebraska Notch

Mount Mansfield State Forest, Underhill Center, Vermont

Type of trail:	⬭ ▬
Also used by:	Backcountry skiers, hikers
Distance:	4.3 miles
Terrain:	Hilly
Trail difficulty:	More difficult
Surface quality:	Ungroomed, but packed by use
Food and facilities:	There are no facilities near the loop; winter campers use Twin Brooks Tenting Area; a brook is water source, bring a filter to treat water. For food, stock up before you go; there are two general stores at Underhill Center—Underhill Country Store (802–899–4056) and Wells Corner Market (802–899–2418)—for last minute items.
Phone numbers:	Vermont Department of Forests, Parks and Recreation in Essex Junction on West Street, (802) 879–6565.

Vermont's most famous face may be its highest peak—Mount Mansfield. At 4,393 feet it's ridge looks a bit like a human profile, and specific features are given names of human parts, like nose, chin, forehead, and even Adam's apple.

Though this loop does not climb to the summit of the peak, it does utilize the Long Trail, which leads to the top. The Long Trail is a 270-mile-long hiking trail that runs from the Massachusetts-Vermont line to the Canadian border. Maintained by the Green Mountain Club, it has some 175 miles of side trails, too. The Long Trail is actually the oldest long-distance hiking trail in the country, according to the Green Mountain Club.

> ## Directions at a glance
>
> 0.0 Leave on the Nebraska Notch Trail.
>
> 1.7 Turn left on the Long Trail.
>
> 3.1 Turn left on the Overland Cross-Country Ski Trail and return 1.2 miles to the parking area.

In winter sections of the trail are used for snowshoeing and skiing.

Three trails make up this loop in the Mount Mansfield State Forest: Nebraska Notch Trail, the Long Trail, and the Overland Cross-Country Ski Trail. As a snowshoe trip, the loop is a moderate undertaking. To complete the entire loop as a backcounry skier, it is best to be at least at an intermediate level.

The Nebraska Notch Trail leaves the trailhead by a sign near the parking lot and is a long, moderate climb. At about 0.1 mile the Overland

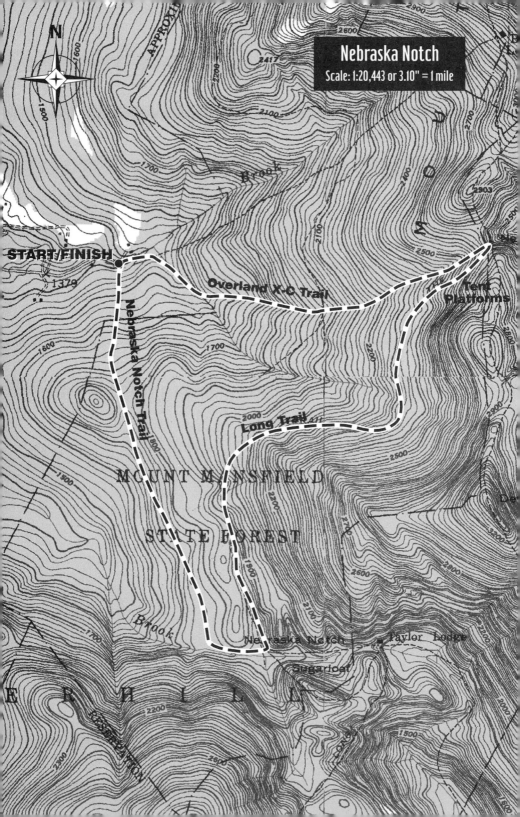

Cross-Country Ski Trail enters left, but the blue-blazed Nebraska Notch continues upward along a wide swath. Streams flow trailside. You'll cross a log bridge. There is a bit of relief by a clearing where you can spot the 2,979-foot Mount Clark. Nebraska Notch Trail descends rather nicely along a brook before you cross a bridge (put up by the Underhill/Jericho Boy Scouts in 1991) to the left. Notice the first of a series of beaver ponds. Cross the bridge and begin a steep ascent to a trail junction. You can make a short side trip at the junction with the Long Trail by making a right and heading 0.4 mile through the glacial cirque and walls of Nebraska Notch to the privately owned Taylor Lodge on the Lake Mansfield Trail (a private trout fishing club). Vistas of Lake Mansfield and beyond are the rewards.

Turn left on the white-blazed Long Trail at the sign and head north. The trail rolls along the west side of Mount Dewey; its huge boulders with icy claws are in the distance. It is narrow in places, and there are a few wet spots, including two brooks at 2.9 miles into the trip, and then one about 0.1 mile later. The first two brooks you reach are quick and steep. After the second brook you'll reach the Twin Brooks Tenting Area. Soon after the area, the red-blazed Overland Cross-Country Ski Trail enters. Thanks go to the Civilian Conservation Corps, which built the Overland back in the 1930s. Turn left and begin the long, winding, and mostly wide descent. The Underhill Ski Trail soon enters to the right, but stay left on Overland. The trail will cross a couple of brooks and drainages.

After about 1.1 miles the Overland rejoins the Nebraska Notch Trail and returns to the parking area.

How to get there

From I–89 north take exit 15 east. Travel through Essex Junction, Essex Center, and Jericho. In Underhill Flats turn right at 13.2 miles on River Road. In Underhill Center, at 16.4 miles, turn right on Stevensville Road and follow it about a mile to a skier parking area on the left. The Maple Leaf Farm is a landmark. Stevensville Road continues about another mile to the trailhead for Nebraska Notch, but it is only suitable for four-wheel drive vehicles. This trip begins there from the well-signed trailhead. Sign in.

A snowshoer signs the log book at the trailhead for the Nebraska Notch Trail.

Indian Brook Park Loop
Essex, Vermont

Type of trail:	(symbols)
Also used by:	Hikers
Distance:	Nearly 2.0 miles
Terrain:	Flat, a few hills
Trail difficulty:	Easiest
Surface quality:	Ungroomed but packed
Food and facilities:	There are no winter facilities at the conservation area; the nearest food is in Essex Junction: a supermarket (Hannaford) near the junction of Routes 15 and 289. After the jaunt try Martone's Market (802–878–8163) on Main Street, Essex Junction, for deli.
Phone numbers:	Essex Parks and Recreation Department, (802) 878–1342.

Circling Indian Brook Reservoir is like taking a leisurely stroll. It is not uncommon to meet locals out for a walk with their dogs on a warm winter afternoon. The trail, which goes around the finger-shaped lake, is never far from the shore, offering panoramas of the frozen water and its various bays. Located in Essex, outside of Vermont's largest city, Burlington, the nearly 2-mile-long loop is easy to ski or snowshoe. Those on skis will find some of the hills exhilarating as well, as the trail rolls up and down in a few sections.

The 66-acre lake is a conservation and public recreation area on a total of 574 acres. The dam, evident near the lake's edge, was built in 1957 so the lake could serve as a water supply.

The counterclockwise loop begins at the summer boat launch area. There is no sign marking the trail, though blue arrows do point the way along the path. The trail initally skirts the shore as it rolls through the forest. Up to the right are rocks that tumbled down when a glacier moved through the area. The trail widens out at about 0.3 mile as it passes by an inlet called Scout's Point. This section of the loop is a road that is lined in parts by an old stone wall. The trail leaves the view of the lake and

Directions at a glance

0.0 Leave the unmarked trail-head along the reservoir shores.

0.3 The trail bears right at a blue arrow.

0.6 Turn left at blue arrow.

1.1 Junction with McGee Road. Turn right at arrow.

1.7 Cross road by dam.

1.8 Turn left on Indian Brook Road back to parking area.

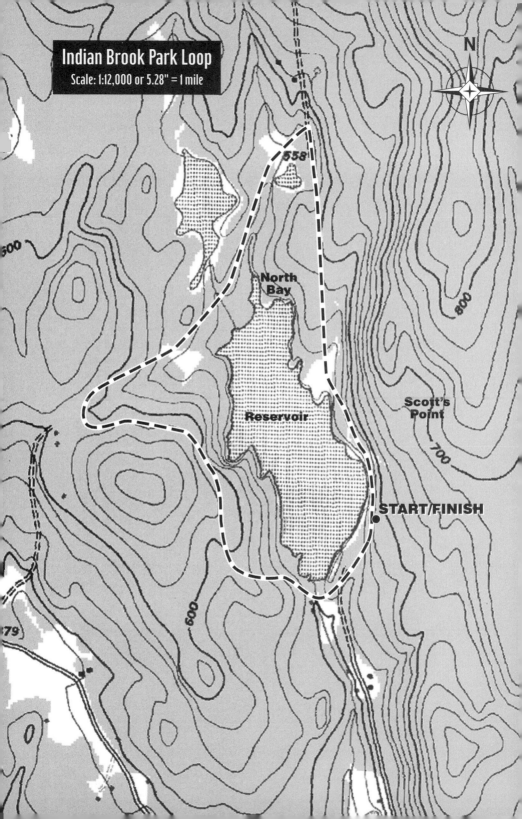

begins to ascend here. The loop takes a big left turn at about the 0.6-mile mark and meanders through a marshy area at the northern tip of the lake, called appropriately enough North Bay.

The northern edge of the loop is hilly as it climbs up on a bit of ridge before rolling back down and toying with coming near and away from the water's edge.

At 1.1 miles there is a signed junction with McGee Road. The trail bears to the left, following the edge of the water. After the junction cross over a tributary and start a gentle ascent away from the water. Glide down as the trail of softwoods and evergreens offers you a view of Thunder Bay. As the trail nears its end, it leaves the woods and comes out near the reservoir's dam. Here it seems to peter out. But it's easy to get back to the trailhead. Cross over the road by the cul-de-sac, and then you'll see the familiar Indian Brook Road. Just turn left and follow the road back to the trailhead.

How to get there

From I–89 north take exit 15 and travel east on Route 15 through Essex Junction. Cross over I–289 and make the first left on Old Stage Road. Make a second left on Indian Brook Road. Follow road into the park and bear right. The road ends at the trailhead near a number of boulders. In summer this is the boat launch. The trailhead is to the left of the rocks.

Sam's Run

Craftsbury Outdoor Center, Craftsbury Common, Vermont

Type of trail:	
Distance:	7.2 miles
Terrain:	Rolling, steep sections
Trail difficulty:	Most difficult
Surface quality:	Groomed, single-tracked, skate lane
Food and facilities:	Cross-country ski and snowshoe rentals, lessons, a wax room, and snacks for the trails are available at the Nordic ski center; overnight accommodations—two lodges and three cabins—are also available. Breakfast, lunch, and dinner are served at the Craftsbury Outdoor Center; you can find sanwiches and last minute items for the trail at the Craftsbury General Store, (802) 586–2811.
Phone numbers:	Craftsbury Outdoor Center, (800) 729–7751.

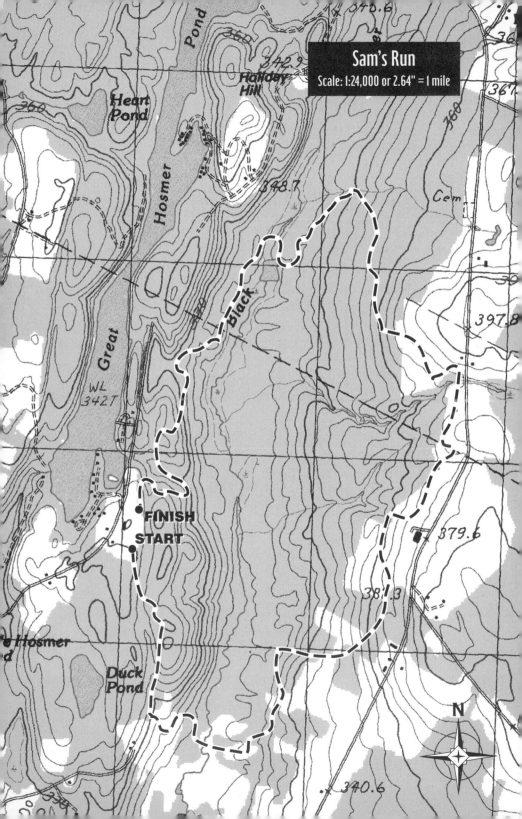

The far reaches of Vermont's Northeast Kingdom are home to the 65 miles of cross-country ski trails at the Craftsbury Outdoor Center. The trails, open to snowshoers, who also have about a 6-mile network just for themselves, wander through the woods with views of rippling hills or drop down into the picture-perfect village of Craftsbury Common, with its snow-covered town green, white homes, and Black River Valley vistas.

A rustic yet charming atmosphere pervades the Nordic network. Ski through a farm meadow with a classic New England red barn, and then wind though the tranquility of the woods and stop at a beaver pond.

Five trailheads, lettered A through F, are the starting points for the suggested tours. Although many Nordic networks have names for the trails marked along the way, at Craftsbury the trails are just numbered loops and are very easy to follow.

Though Sam's Run, trail 14, is marked as a more difficult loop, it really doesn't feel that way. The 7-plus-mile circuit through open fields, along a flowing river, and through the maples that drip syrup near spring is hilly, with a long, moderate climb. But the beauty of cross-country skiing is ripping down the nicely groomed boulevards after those pushes. The trail also undergoes a bit of a personality change. At the onset wide open fields dominate the scenery. Then the route heads into the forest, playfully twisting its way back to the touring center.

Sam's Run was named, not surprisingly, after a man named Sam. The story goes that Sam was looking for Ruthie's Run, a trail named after a hound dog. Sam got lost, and Sam's Run was the trail he made.

Sam's Run leaves from trailhead B, diagonally behind the outdoor center, by the lesson area. Well marked, Sam's Run begins as a rolling path and a corridor where several other trails start. The first major junction comes after a short climb to Log Landing. Here trail 14 bears to the right through the maples. Continue upward through the coniferous forest and a joyous clearing atop Elinor's Hill, where a gray barn takes up residence and views of distant hills frame the Black River Valley below.

From Elinor's Hill there is an open, winding, fairly steep drop to the valley floor. Cross the Black River on a bridge by a beaver pond. From

Directions at a glance

0.0 Leave from trailhead B and follow signs for trail 14.

0.1 Turn left at sign for trail 14.

1.0 Turn left at sign for trail 14 Elinor's Hill.

2.9 Continue straight at merge with trails 13 and 15.

5.8 Turn left at junction and continue on trail 14.

7.0 Turn left at junction and continue on trail 14.

A farm meadow and a rustic barn await skiers and shoers at Sam's Run.

here Sam's Run begins a long crawl upward, passing through pastures with impressive vistas of the Worcester Range and a nearby hilltop farm. A yellow farmhouse acts like a beacon as the trail parallels the dirt Creek Road. Near the yellow home, the path bears left and skirts an open field before sinking back into the woods for some fast twists and rolls through the pine forest. You pass more beaver ponds in an area where skiers have spotted tracks from bear, moose, and mountain lions. Cross the Black River again and begin another push upward. Some of the center's cabins can be seen high atop the hill. Head up and come out to a clearing where Big Hosmer Lake sits across the road.

Bear left and parallel Lost Nation Road back to the center.

How to get there

From Hardwick follow Route 14 north 8.4 miles and turn right on TH 1 (sign for Craftsbury Outdoor Center). Follow TH 1 about 4.0 miles and make right on TH 7. Travel TH 7 for 1.3 miles and turn right on TH 12 (Lost Nation Road) and follow it to the Craftsbury Outdoor Center. The way from Route 14 is well signed.

Stowe Recreation Path

Stowe, Vermont

Type of trail:	◉ ▬
Also used by:	Walkers
Distance:	5.5 miles one way
Terrain:	Flat
Trail difficulty:	Easiest
Surface quality:	Partially groomed, skier tracked
Food and facilities:	Rental shops on Mountain Road in Stowe have cross-country skis and snowshoes. One is Action Outfitters, (802) 253–7975. A number of restaurants can be accessed by the Recreation Path; a grocery store, Grand Union, is off Route 100 (Maple Street).
Phone numbers:	Stowe Chamber of Commerce, (802) 253–7321; police emergency, 911.

Stowe and skiing go hand-in-hand. Though the area is known for its diverse alpine slopes, four groomed cross-country ski networks, and miles of backcountry adventures, as well as home to the state's highest peak, there are those days when simple and scenic will do. On those days, the Stowe Recreation Path is the answer.

Flatish and free, the paved path constructed in the early 1980s is a 5.5-mile-long white greenway, utilized by cross-country skiers, snowshoers, and walkers in winter. The small-town atmosphere of Stowe is evident along the path that meanders between the flowing waters of the West Branch River and Stowe's commercial Mountain Road (Route 108). Stowe is a hip place. Yes, dogs are allowed on the path. However, how many other communities make this request of dog owners: "Please suggest to your dogs that they use the woods (the pavement is nicer when kept clean)." The good thing about the path is that it is used by locals. When playing the visitor, locals are your best resource. Be nice and maybe they'll let you in on local skiing and après-ski secrets.

Directions at a glance

0.0 Leave from the trailhead by the Stowe Community Church.

3.0 The parking area by Luce Hill Road.

3.8 The parking area by Mountain Road.

5.5 The path ends by the covered bridge and Brook Road parking area.

5. Return along same route.

Stowe Recreation Path
Scale: 1:28,170 or 2.25" = 1 mile

The path begins beside the charming white Stowe Community Church and ends by a red covered bridge spanning the river. In between the greenway winds through and around open fields, woods, quaint inns, incredible vistas of Mount Mansfield, and farms. Take a backpack and stop to shop along the way—the path accesses some of the stores along Mountain Road. Lunch is also a possibility because the path takes you past menus offering everything from fast burgers to prime rib and lobster. Have fun choosing.

The path doesn't take you far from civilization, and certainly the cars on Mountain Road will remind of you of that, but the path does offer its quiet and pastoral moments.

The path begins by the Stowe Community Church, arguably the most photographed building in town. The church was constructed for $12,000 in 1863. Almost immediately, you cross the first of ten bridges along the path. Whether you take off your winter equipment to cross is determined by the type of equipment you have, your confidence, and the amount of snow on that day. Take off your equipment for the road crossings you encounter.

Ski past the scenery along the West River and look up to Mount Mansfield, the highest peak in the state.

There are many fine vistas, and the views of the farm and Mount Mansfield from the Thompson Park bridge are spectacular.

It is not necessary to ski the entire length of the path and return, though that makes a fine outing. Four public parking areas allow users access to the path at different spots, making the trip an out-and-back-to-the-car experience. Aside from the area at the church, the others are on Luce Hill Road (across from the Snowdrift Motel), off Mountain Road by the Alpenrose, and at the end of the path by the red covered bridge on Brook Road.

How to get there

From I–89 take exit 10 and follow Route 100 north about 11 miles to Stowe Village. Route 100 becomes Main Street, and the Recreation Path leaves from the Stowe Community Church.

Slayton Pasture Cabin/Haul Road Loop

Trapp Family Lodge, Stowe, Vermont

Type of trail:	▬ ≺ ●
Distance:	7.2 miles
Terrain:	Flat, rolling, hilly
Trail difficulty:	More difficult
Surface quality:	Groomed, single track, double track
Food and facilities:	Rentals (cross-country and snowshoe), lessons, rest rooms, gift shop, a wax room, and more are available at the ski touring center. The Slayton Pasture Cabin, near the loop's halfway mark, is an ideal lunch spot.
Phone numbers:	The Trapp Family Lodge, (802) 253–5719.

The hills above Stowe are alive with cross-country skiing and snowshoeing at the Trapp Family Lodge. The 35 miles of groomed trails (snowshoers are welcome on all of them plus about 4 miles of their own) is at the heart of Stowe's extensive network of some 90 miles of groomed trails. The four centers—Trapp, Edson Hill Manor, Topnotch, and Stowe Mountain Touring Center—in the shadows of impressive Mount Mansfield, are interconnected.

The upscale Trapp Family Lodge takes credit for being the first commercial Nordic center in the United States. In 1968 Johannes von Trapp, whose family inspired the film *Sound of Music,* started out with a few wooden skis and a Norwegian instructor. The Austrian expatriates never looked back as the resort has grown to attract some 30,000 skiers per year.

> ## Directions at a glance
>
> 0.0 From the ski center take Sugar Road.
>
> 1.2 Turn right on Parizo Trail.
>
> 2.4 Turn left on Cabin Trail. The Slayton Pasture Cabin is at 3.0 miles.
>
> 3.0 Take the Haul Road.
>
> 6.9 Haul Road becomes Luce Trail. Follow it 0.3 mile to the ski touring center.

Located up in the hills with panoramic views of the Stowe Valley and surrounding mountains, the wide, neatly groomed trails of the network are novice and intermediate friendly. Beginners can stay near the ski center in the lower elevations, making an easy loop along the tree-lined Sugar Road to Russell Knoll Track.

But those seeking more of a challenge and impressive mountain views can try their skill on the Slayton Pasture Cabin/Haul Road Loop. There is something satisfying and homey about stopping in a rustic log

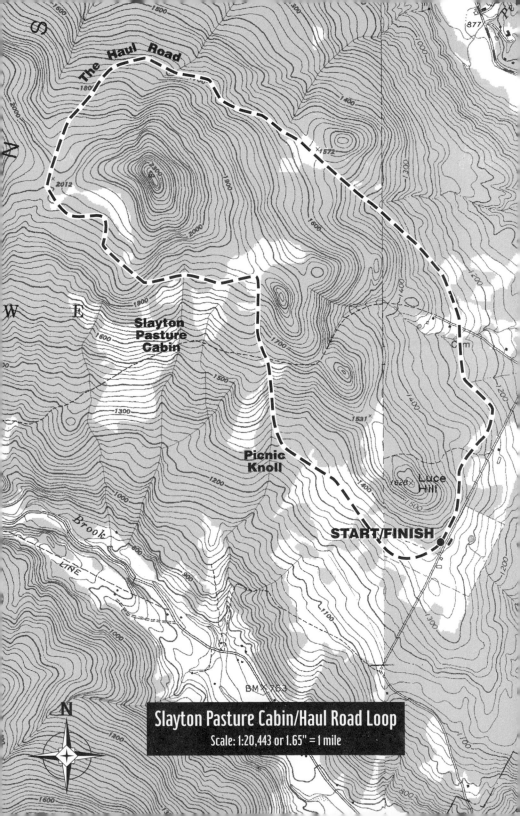

The Haul Road

S

A

2000

2012

W

E

Slayton
Pasture
Cabin

1900

600

1300

Brook

LINE

Picnic
Knoll

1200

1000

900

BM × 763

×1572

1600

1700

1500

1531

1400

1628 ×

Luce
Hill

1500

START/FINISH

Cem

1200

1100

1300

N

Slayton Pasture Cabin/Haul Road Loop
Scale: 1:20,443 or 1.65" = 1 mile

cabin in the woods to rest and refuel with hot drinks, soups, and snacks. Just before the midway point, the Slayton Pasture Cabin provides that, with a porch for bird-watching, too.

Instant vistas await users of the network—the Green Mountains over Lake Mansfield are the backdrop for the ski center.

From the center the loop begins at the gentle Sugar Road. Double tracked with a skate lane, Sugar Road is a pleasant and easy corridor through the woods. The ascent is extremely gradual, and an occasional bench welcomes rest and reflection. The cover of the woods gives way to a clearing called Picnic Knoll at the end of Sugar Road. From here you can spot Camel's Hump, wide and white, and the 4,083-foot Mount Ellen on a clear day.

The Slayton Pasture Cabin is an ideal lunch spot for skiers and shoers in need of a break.

The work begins at Picnic Knoll. Slayton Pasture Cabin is on the slopes of Round Top Mountain at an elevation of 2,100 feet. To get there you have to cover 700 feet of elevation gain in a couple of miles. The most popular route is the Parizo Trail. (Actually there are two Parizo Trails: One goes up; the other, down.) During the moderate climb with its few steep pitches, skiers don't have to be concerned about a smiling downhiller impeding their grunt. The trail crosses Old County Road and links up to the Cabin Trail, which rolls upward to the cabin. Stop at the cabin to rest up. That was 3 miles.

The Haul Road, a logging road, is a 4.0-mile gradual descent back to the touring center. Not too long after leaving the cabin on the Haul Road look for the jaw-dropping northern view of the alpine slopes of Smugglers' Notch and the dramatic Elephant's Head ledge. Round the trail some more and gaze east to the Worcester Range at the prominent Mount Elmore and 3,293-foot Mount Worcester. The Haul Road returns to the woods and winds down, offering a few clearings along the way. Cross Old County Road (sometimes you have to take off your skis) where 3,538-foot Hunger Mountain and Camel's Hump provide excellent vistas. Lower Haul Road links to the Luce Trail, which leads back to the ski center.

How to get there

From I–89 take exit 10 and follow Route 100 north 7.0 miles to Moscow Road. Turn left. Follow Moscow Road 1.6 miles to Barrows Road and turn right. After 2.0 miles turn left on Trapp Hill Road. Follow it 1.0 mile to the Trapp Family Lodge.

Robert Frost Interpretive Trail
Ripton, Vermont

Type of trail:	(icons)
Also used by:	Hikers
Distance:	1.0 mile
Terrain:	Flat
Trail difficulty:	Easiest
Surface quality:	Ungroomed
Food and facilities:	Pit toilet, guest book, and donation request are at the trailhead. The general store in Ripton has sandwiches for a quick post-tour bite. Nearby Middlebury has a selection of restaurants.
Phone numbers:	U.S. Forest Service's Middlebury Ranger District, (802) 388–4362; Vermont State Police, (802) 244–8781.

The poet Robert Frost drank in inspiration from the woods, rivers, and mountains of Vermont and New Hampshire. Whether it be the white, supple branches of a bending birch or swift, flowing waters of a frigid river, the images found in the words of a Frost poem can be seen from the short, easy, and soothing Robert Frost Interpretive Trail.

The loop, located in the Green Mountain National Forest, is unique in that several of Frost's poems are mounted on placards along the way ("The Road not Taken," "Winter Eden," "Pasture"). Wooden benches have been placed near some of the poems as if to invite introspection. Blueberries and huckleberries at the far end of a field await new life in spring. The South Branch of the Middlebury River crosses here, and there is even a boardwalk with benches so snowshoers and skiers can pause at a frozen beaver pond. In the silence listen to the waters of the river. Not only are Frost's poems on display, but signs also indicate what types of trees are in the area, like beech, pine, birch, spruce, fir, and alder. Visitors can also learn about the wildflowers that grow here in the nonsnow months.

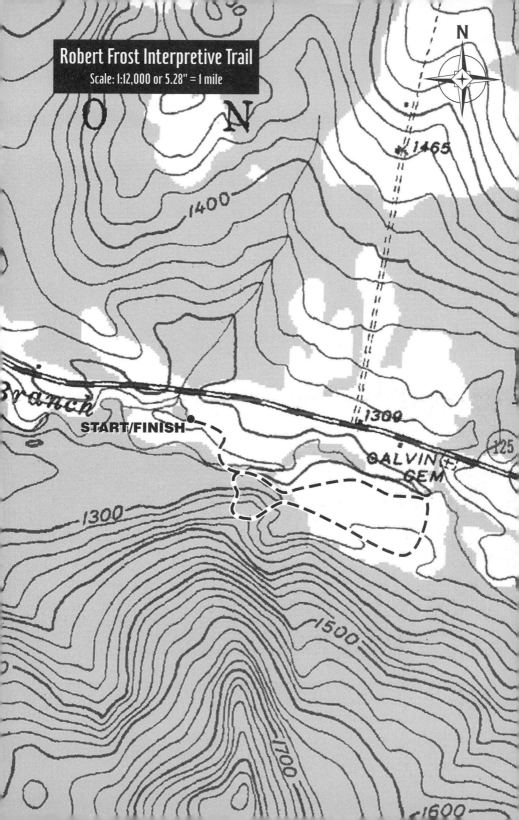

The Forest Service uses prescribed fire to maintain the old fields and meadows along the way, preserve the scenic value of the area, and regenerate vegetation growth. The burns take place every three or four years. From the fields Fire Tower Hill, Breadloaf Mountain, Battell Mountain, Kirby Peak, and Burnt Hill provide a panorama. Frost lived in a small cabin in Ripton (about a mile from the trailhead) for twenty-three summers. Because of Frost's long association with the area (dubbed "Robert Frost Country" in 1983 by then Governor Richard Snelling, it was thought Frost's work should be commemorated. His imprint is found in many places in Vermont, from a mountain that bears his name to the stretch of Route 125 from Middlebury Gap to Hancock named Robert Frost Memorial Drive. The trail was dedicated on August 28, 1976. Frost was a Vermont poet laurate. Those not familiar with his writings might find an appreciation for them on this trail and in this setting.

Directions at a glance

0.0 Leave the trailhead, following the sign that points the way.

0.2 Bear right at arrow that says "trail."

0.3 Cross the bridge over the river and bear right, then left around the wooden bench.

0.6 Follow sign that indicates Frost Trail.

0.9 Bear right at sign with arrow pointing to parking.

The interpretive signs, easy terrain, benches, and views make this an ideal showshoe for children. The signs turn the loop into a game and benches provide rest. After this loop you might enjoy this stanza from the Frost poem, "Stopping by Woods on a Snowy Evening":

The woods are lovely, dark, and deep,

But I have promises to keep

And miles to go before I sleep

And miles to go before I sleep.

How to get there
The trailhead is on Route 125 about 4 miles west of Middlebury Gap or 2 miles east of Ripton.

Camel's Hump View Trail
Camel's Hump State Park, Waterbury, Vermont

Type of trail:	═══ ▬▬▬
Also used by:	Hikers
Distance:	Nearly 1.0 mile
Terrain:	Flat gentle hill
Trail difficulty:	Easiest
Surface quality:	Ungroomed, skier packed
Food and facilities:	There are no facilities at the trailhead. For food Waterbury has a Grand Union on Main Street, or try Arvads (802–244–8973) also on Main Street.
Phone numbers:	Vermont State Department of Forest, Parks and Recreation Office, Waterbury, (802) 241–3678 for more information.

It is not too often the word *easy* is used in conjunction with Camel's Hump. Vermont's hunchback of winter, the 4,063-foot-high peak is one of the state's most prominent features and is also a summit devoid of any development, like ski lifts or antennas. From the gentle and welcoming Camel's Hump View Trail, skiers and snowshoers can pause on a bench and take in the views of the mountain a few miles away.

Camel's Hump View is a relatively new wheelchair-accessible path built in the early 1990s. Because it must accommodate wheelchairs during the nonsnow months, it is wide and its grade is gentle. This 0.8-mile loop is a very easy excursion, ideal for the family. The kids will enjoy trying to ski or snowshoe from bench to bench, crossing a bridge, looking for the work done by woodpeckers, or trying to identify the animal tracks—like those of a snowshoe hare—in the snow. The benches are also good spots for a lunch.

Directions at a glance

0.0 Leave the trailhead and follow the blue-blazed Camel's Hump View Trail.

0.3 The Ridley Crossing Cross-Country Ski Trail enters right. Continue to the left, following the blue blazes around and back to the trailhead.

Camel's Hump State Park is in the northern half of Vermont's Green Mountains. The park had its beginnings in 1911 when a man named Colonel Joseph Battell of Middlebury donated 1,000 acres of land, including the summit of Camel's Hump, to preserve the view from his home. Since then the park has grown to about 24,000 acres.

Camel's Hump View Trail
Scale: 1:24,000 or 2.64" = 1 mile

START/FINISH

MONROE

STATE PARK

CAMELS HUMP

STATE FOREST

The Camel's Hump View Trail begins at a well-marked trailhead. The loop can be done in either direction, but we'll go counterclockwise to enjoy the downhill near the end of the loop. Blue blazes mark the way as the trail begins by the rushing waters of Sinnott Brook. It's not too long before you reach the first bench. Stop to admire the view of Camel's Hump off in the distance. Near the midway mark Camel's Hump View intersects with the Ridley Crossing Cross-Country Ski Trail. A possible side trip for better skiers, the ski trail, marked with blue diamonds, is sandwiched between Ridley and Sinnott Brooks. At 0.9 miles it reaches the Beaver Meadow Trail, a section of the Vermont Association of Snow Travelers network of snowmobile trails. (One can either return to Camel's Hump View, or, by turning right on Beaver Meadow, go on for more than a mile before coming back to Camel's Hump Road, where a right turn and a short walk brings you back to the Camel's View Trailhead.

On Camel's Hump View the trail snakes near Sinnott Brook and then begins to head down on the other side of the brook. More benches mark the way. You see Camel's Hump through the evergreens as the trail descends and banks to the left. The familiar parking lot is soon ahead, but first head over the bridge built by the On Top School in 1993. There is a final bench here before you reach the parking lot.

How to get there

From I–89 take exit 10. Travel on Route 2 east 0.1 mile and make a right on Winooski Street. Travel about 0.5 mile and cross over a bridge. Turn right after the bridge. This is Duxbury Road. Follow it 4.0 miles and make a left on Camel's Hump Road. The trailhead is about 3.5 miles down the road.

Burrows Trail

Camel's Hump State Park, Huntington Center, Vermont

Type of trail:	⬤⬤⬤
Also used by:	Backcountry skiers, hikers
Distance:	4.8 miles
Terrain:	Hilly, last pitch is above treeline
Trail difficulty:	Most difficult
Surface quality:	Ungroomed, but packed
Food and facilities:	There are no facilities at the trailhead. Jaque's Country Store and Deli (802–434–2674) in Huntington, on Main Road, is for last minute items and the post-trip sandwich; later consider the buffet at the House of Tang on River Street, Montpelier (802–223–6020).
Phone numbers:	Call the Essex Junction office of the Vermont State Department of Forests, Parks and Recreation (802–879–6565) or the department headquarters in Waterbury (802–241–3678) for information.

The Green Mountain Club estimates some 20,000 people ascend to the summit of Camel's Hump each year. The hike to its 4,083-foot summit is popular in summer, and snowshoeing and skiing on the mountain have been gaining momentum during winter. Ascending Camel's Hump is a trip that should be well planned and done with caution. Clear skies and calm winds can change immediately to 40-mile-per-hour gusts and whiteout conditions. Knowing the forecast is of prime importance.

On Camel's Hump the winter enthusiast is above the treeline and exposed to wind. Icy and windswept conditions can haunt a summit, and the open ridges make snowshoes impractical. Crampons are better.

Backcountry skiers can combine skiing and snowshoeing on this one.

Directions at a glance

0.0 Leave to the right of the signboard on the Burrows Trail.

2.1 Turn right at junction and travel 0.3 to the summit.

Return via the same route.

Many favor the section of the Burrows Trail featured in this trip as a skinup, ski-down experience.

The summit of the double-humped mountain in Camel's Hump State Park supports Arctic-alpine vegetation. Many of the plants are on the state's endangered species list. Travel only on the marked trails to protect the fragile ecosystem. Though winter sometimes hangs on in Vermont,

and snow might still be found at higher elevations, the trails to Camel's Hump usually are closed by mid-April for a few weeks to minimize damage during spring meltdown. Heed this rule.

The blue-blazed Burrows Trail, which leaves from a plowed dirt parking area, scales the western side of the mountain. Enter the woods and proceed to the signboard where winter recreationalists are encouraged to sign in. The trailhead is also a starting point for another way up the mountain. Though longer, it is possible to snowshoe up to the summit by taking the Burrows–Forest City Connector Trail for 0.1 mile to a left on the Forest City Trail to Wind Gap, where a left on the Long Trail heads up to the summit.

The Burrows Trail is initially wide and is a moderate climb in the beginning, passing a bench with a view looking down on a rushing stream.

The Burrows Trail waits for fresh tracks on the way up or down Camel's Hump.

As the trail progresses it narrows as groves of evergreen trees enter the landscape. The Burrows Trail will also get progressively steeper until it reaches a clearing some 0.3 mile from the summit. The flat clearing is a spot where many trails intersect. Turning right leads to the treeless, rocky summit.

The summit is a stunning, unspoiled area. From it New Hampshire's White Mountains lay to the east. Vermont's Green Mountains spread along a north-south corridor. The Adirondacks in New York appear in the western sky.

From here descend along the same route some 2,000 feet back to the trailhead.

How to get there

From I–89 take exit 11 and then Route 2 east to Richmond. Turn left on Bridge Street and follow it to Huntington Center. Turn left on Camel's Hump Road and follow the road 3.5 miles to the trailhead. Four-wheel drive is suggested for the last mile. If not available, park by the lower unplowed trailhead and walk 0.7 to the winter trailhead.

Faulkner Trail
Woodstock, Vermont

Type of trail:	⬭
Also used by:	Hikers
Distance:	1.6 miles one way, 3.2 miles round-trip
Terrain:	Hilly
Trail difficulty:	Easiest, except for the last 0.1 mile, which is steep and rocky
Surface quality:	Ungroomed
Food and facilities:	There are no facilities. In Woodstock there is a Grand Union on Route 4. After the trip try Bentleys Restaurant on Elm Street, (802) 457–3232. Skiers wishing to access the summit of Mount Tom can do so via the Sleigh Ride Trail groomed and maintained by the Woodstock Ski Touring Center. That trail is 2.0 miles each way. Snowshoers are also welcome on the Sleigh Ride Trail. There is an access fee for that trail.
Phone numbers:	Woodstock Ski Touring Center, (802) 457–6674. (The center offers an extensive network of mapped and marked trails that are immediately adjacent. The center itself is located a half mile south of the village green on Route 106.)

The top of Mount Tom's south peak in winter offers a splendid panorama of central Vermont and the upper Connecticut River Valley into New Hampshire. Even from a wooden semicircular bench by Woodstock's illuminating Christmas star, you can see the quaintness that is Woodstock. Mountains, hills, and neat farms are off in the distance. Down below, like a miniature town from a childhood railroad display, Woodstock is alive. Smoke rises from the woodstoves and fireplaces. The Ottauquechee River cuts its path through town. The Federal-style, immaculate homes that line the village green appear diminutive. Even the covered bridge in town is visible. The mountain top offers a clear glimpse into the way Rockefeller money has preserved both history and land in Woodstock.

Directions at a glance

0.0 Leave Mountain Avenue on the unsigned Faulkner Trail by the stone wall at one end of Faulkner Park and enter the woods. Follow the yellow-blazed trail to the left.

1.2 Turn left on the Faulkner Trail (there's a sign). The Link Trail enters from the right.

1.5 Bench with an open view.

1.6 Top of Mount Tom's south peak.

Return the same way.

N

PATH

888

1000

Mt. Tom

700

River Street
Cem

701

700

697

START/FINISH

Faulkner
Park

900

900

800

Faulkner Trail
Scale: 1:12,000 or 5.28" = 1 mile

From the summit of Mount Tom in Woodstock, the views of Vermont are stunning.

To snowshoe up 1,240-foot Mount Tom in winter is to have an Old World experience. The yellow-blazed Faulkner Trail is a series of switchbacks that zigzag up to the top where an old carriage road loops around. Follow the circular path and be treated to views of the village, Killington Peak, Mount Ascutney, Mount Peg, and the mountains of the Granite State. The grade up the Faulkner Trail is very gentle, and the many benches placed along the way, though some may be covered with snow, are places to rest. Huge boulders, left behind as the glaciers retreated, call the mountain home. In winter ice clings to the stones with chilling fingers. Stone walls reach out from the snow, and a stone bridge is nearby.

Faulkner Park on Mountain Avenue is obvious but not signed. The unmarked trail begins by a stone wall next to a stunning white home with pond, gazebo, and picnic table. The trail enters the woods by a huge rock, bears left, and immediately begins the switchbacks that make the trail so easy to follow. Though obvious shortcuts present themselves, it is best to stick to the trail. At least on the way up.

After about 1.0 mile the Link Trail enters right by an old railing, and the Faulkner Trail bears to the left. The trail passes large rock faces and the views through the trees are impressive. A wooden bench on a knoll offering vistas of the village and hills marks the 1.5-mile mark.

The next 100 yards to the summit of the south peak is not an easy jaunt. The trail drops quickly and then climbs steeply and narrowly over rocks. A handrail is there for assistance. At the top be sure to head around the carriage road. In winter the Woodstock Ski Touring Center grooms the carriage road as part of its 35 miles of trails. Be courteous and don't snowshoe on the groomed tracks. There is plenty of room for everyone.

To return to the park, return the same way, following the sign that reads MOUNTAIN AVENUE. Carefully descend the path back to the wooden bench. Once there let the fun begin. Use your discretion in romping through the snow on the way back down.

How to get there

Faulker Park is located on Mountain Avenue in Woodstock. There are a number of parking alternatives in winter. Park by the Woodstock village green and walk through the covered bridge on Union Street, crossing River Street and taking a left on Mountain Avenue to Faulkner Park. Or park across the street from the Woodstock Recreation Department in the parking area on Route 4. Walk to the park by turning left on Mountain Avenue to Faulkner Park.

Hogback Trail

Blueberry Hill Nordic Center, Goshen, Vermont

Type of trail:	
Distance:	3.8 miles
Terrain:	Hilly
Trail difficulty:	More difficult
Surface quality:	Groomed, single tracked, skate lane
Food and facilities:	Rentals (skis and snowshoes), lessons, a wax room, retail shop, and cafe are located at the cross-country ski center. There is a trail fee to use the network. For dinner skiers can eat at the Blueberry Hill Inn. Reservations are requested.
Phone numbers:	Blueberry Hill Nordic Center and Inn, (802) 247–6735 or (800) 448–0707.

Vermont's Green Mountain National Forest is divided in two, with northern and southern sections. The 20,000 acres that make up the northern part, called Moosalamoo, is home to more than 60 miles of groomed cross-country ski trails maintained by the Blueberry Inn, Rikert

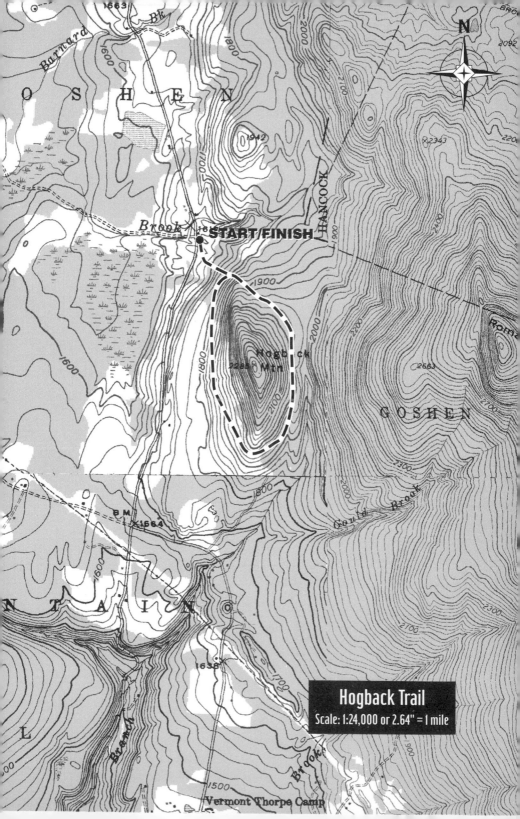

START/FINISH

Hogback Trail
Scale: 1:24,000 or 2.64" = 1 mile

The quaint Blueberry Hill Inn is across the road from the touring center.

Ski Touring Center, and Churchill House Inn, as well as the Catamount Trail and other systems.

The Blueberry Hill Nordic Center is run by one of Vermont's skiing pioneers, Tony Clark. A Brit who grew up in France skiing in the heights of the Alps, this ski mountaineer moved to the area in 1967. At the suggestion of a friend, Johannes Von Trapp, Clark and his then wife opened the center in 1971. The Nordic Center was a ramshackle operation initially, operating on donations. Since then it has grown to have 40 miles of trails (snowshoers are welcome on the network) and is home to a resplendent inn as well. To help skiers and snowshoers get around, trails east of the inn are odd-numbered, and trails to the west are even-numbered. The inn is number one, so if someone loses the way, all they have to do is follow the numbers in descending order back to the center.

Clark has a vision. His legacy is to turn the trail network into a nonprofit foundation and open the system to the public on a no-fee basis, totally supported by Moosalamoo Partnership.

The loop begins with a gentle dip behind the blue inn, which was built in 1813, crossing a brook and then heading upward through the

Directions at a glance

0.0 Leave on the Hogback Trail, which begins behind the inn.

0.3 Turn right at junction 7 where the trail becomes the Zach Osborne Trail.

0.8 Bear left at junction 21.

2.1 Turn left at junction 25.

3.2 Turn left on the Lee Todd Trail at junction 29; follow the trail 0.6 miles back to the inn.

woods. The trail system is constructed in such a way that there are a series of climbs with plateaus, offering a flat respite as a reward for every effort.

The Hogback Trail undergoes a name change and becomes the Zach Osborne Trail after about 0.3 mile. Osborne ran the ski center during the 1994–95 season and worked long, hard hours maintaining the trail he loved. In January 1997, at the age of 39, he died of cancer. The trail was named in his honor.

The trail undulates through land that was once part of the farms in the area. At about midway through the loop, you reach one of the most stunning vistas in the state as the mountains swell in the distance. Leave the shelter of the woods and come out to a clearing where to the west lie the Adirondacks, the Taconics to the south, and the Green Mountains and the Long Trail to the east. The hump that is Hogback rises up like a 2,286-foot-high hunchback. Pause before twisting down for a return to the woods.

After the vista the Halfdan Kuhnle Trail leaves right for a 2.5-mile climb up Romance Mountain. For expert skiers the path is the highest groomed trail in the state. The Hogback Loop continues left with a change of vegetation. Now that they are on the east side of the moun-

tain, skiers follow a ridge that oversees a gully in the spruce and softwood forest.

The trail comes to a junction, number 29, and swings left on the Lee Todd Trail, named after a former ski center director, and finishes back to the inn on a gorgeous downhill.

How to get there

From Brandon follow Route 73 east 4 miles to Forest Road 32. Turn left. Drive 4 miles to the Blueberry Hill Nordic Center.

Waxable skis will make a trek more enjoyable because snow conditions change with the weather and the thermometer.

South Ridge Loop

Mountain Meadows Cross-Country Ski Center, Killington, Vermont

Type of trail:	▬▬ ◄
Distance:	5.4 miles
Terrain:	Hilly, steep sections
Trail difficulty:	Most difficult
Surface quality:	Groomed, single tracked, skate lane
Food and facilities:	Rentals (ski and snowshoes), a wax room, lessons, retail shop, and snack bar are available at Mountain Meadows. For lunch there is Charity's; for dinner, the Wobbly Barn.
Phone numbers:	Mountain Meadows, (800) 221–0598.

Make sure your seatbelts are fastened for a ride on the South Ridge Loop at Mountain Meadows Cross-Country Ski Center in central Vermont. The undulating trail, which opened in December 1997, dances up, down, and around through the woods, by rounded mountains, and past huge boulders and includes a half-mile downhill with exhilarating hairpin turns. Though the trail is virtually new, it has quickly become a favorite among more advanced skiers and may also evolve into the network's banner run.

At one time the area that is Mountain Meadows was a working farm with cattle, sheep, and apple orchards. Though there are still remnants of those days—home foundations and stone walls throughout the northern section of the network—the 37 miles of groomed trails are now within sight of the alpine slopes of Killington and Pico. Snowshoers are not allowed on the ski trails but have their own 6 miles of trails to explore.

Unique to Mountain Meadows is a color-coded trail system. The entire network is composed of loops. Instead of having trail signs with numbers or names, the signs are color coded. Want to do a loop? Just follow its color. Borrowing an idea from our Canadian neighbors, Mountain Meadows also posts distances in descending order back to the touring center. As a loop progresses, the distance is posted at one kilometer intervals, so skiers know how far it is back to the center. These two elements save skiers from having to think too much.

The ski begins with an easy downhill to the frozen shores of Kent Pond (also known as Kent Lake), which is rimmed by hills. Ski over a small portion of the lakeshore before entering the woods and traversing rolling terrain. A short climb of about 100 vertical feet eventually flattens out and leads skiers to a picnic table, covered in snow in winter. Here the roller coaster ride begins. Mountain Meadows doesn't pull punches

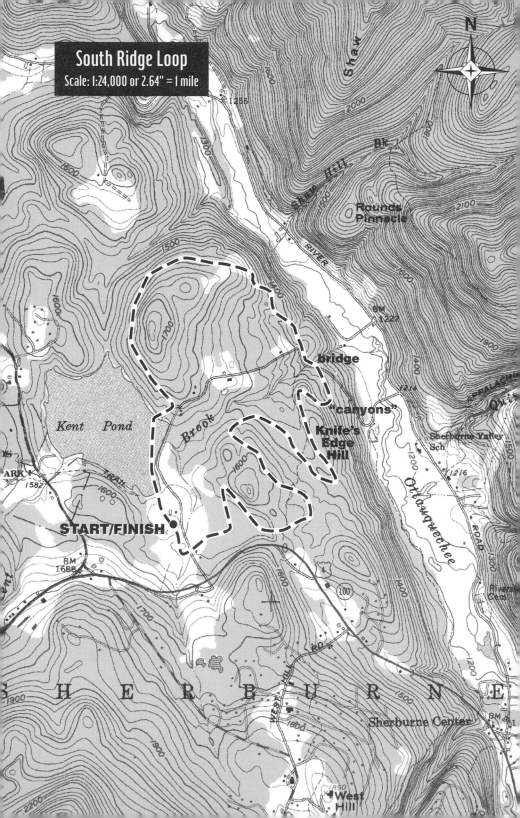

South Ridge Loop
Scale: 1:24,000 or 2.64" = 1 mile

N

Shaw Hill

RIVER

Rounds Pinnacle

BM 1222

bridge

"canyons"

Knife's Edge Hill

Sherburne Valley Sch

1216

Ottauquechee

ROAD

Riverse Cem

Kent Pond

Brook

START/FINISH

BM 1688

100

80

SHERBURNE

WEST HILL

Sherburne Center

BM

West Hill

ARK

BM 1582

about its terrain. Signs warn skiers that if they aren't confident on their boards, don't try it. The rip-roaring descent twists and turns through the old apple orchards. The rounded peaks of the River Road Valley serve as a backdrop seen through the trees.

Directions at a glance

0.0 Leave from behind the touring center on the South Ridge Trail or brown loop.

0.5 Turn right at the brown-colored sign.

0.6 Turn left at the brown-colored sign marked E.

1.8 Bear left at the brown-colored sign marked L.

2.5 Cross Thundering Brook Road and pick up the trail on the other side.

5.2 Cross Thundering Brook Road and pick up the trail for 0.2 mile back to the touring center.

The long downhill ends by crossing Thundering Brook Road where it's a fifty-fifty shot whether you should take off your skis. The trail picks up on the other side of the road and parallels the pristine Thundering Brook for a short spell. (Though they aren't seen on this ski, the falls upstream are the second highest in the state.)

Up and down, like the huge swells of a stormy sea, the trail moves through the forest in a series of switchbacks. Some sections are rather steep, like an area dubbed the "Canyon" because of its resemblence to one. Another hill sure to make skiers use the herringbone technique is the one named "Knife's Edge," which takes skiers up on a razorback under a tall pine grove.

A sweeping turn brings skiers out into a marsh with cat o'nine tails poking through the snow and the ski slopes up ahead. The touring center is in sight, and it's only a short distance back to it.

How to get there

From the intersection of Routes 100 and 4 in Killington, follow Route 4 one-quarter mile east past the access road to Killington. Turn left on Thundering Brook Road to Mountain Meadows.

Merck Forest and Farmland Center's Birch Pond Loop

Rupert, Vermont

Type of trail:	▬▬ ◉
Also used by:	Hikers
Distance:	3.5 miles
Terrain:	Flat to hilly
Trail difficulty:	Easiest
Surface quality:	Ungroomed, but skier tracked
Food and facilities:	Pop in to the Joy Green Visitor Center at the Merck Forest and Farmland Center before heading out. There are rest rooms, water, and snacks. Cabins are available for overnight use for a fee. Nearby Manchester has everything you want in terms of groceries, rentals, and restaurants. In Manchester try Candeleros on Main Street for Mexican food, (802) 362–0836. Cross-country ski and snowshoe rentals are at the Mountain Goat, Route 7A (Historic Main Street) in Manchester, (802) 362–5159.
Phone numbers:	Merck Forest and Farmland Center, (802) 394–7836; Rupert Police, (802) 394–7778.

Ski by a wide, open field with views of the hills of New York and stop to watch horses eat some hay. Snowshoe by a handsome farm and watch the cattle eating. Enter into a maple grove and see the taps in the trees for the collection of sap, which will be boiled down into syrup.

These and other experiences await visitors to the Merck Forest and Farmland Center in southern Vermont. (As employees are quick to note, the center is not affiliated with the Merck Company.) Located on 3,130 acres of hilltop working farm and forest land, the center is an environmental educational organization in the Taconic Range. Recreational and educational programs abound on its 28 miles of snowshoe and cross-country ski trails.

This nonprofit organization looks to the community for support, and it welcomes memberships and donations. There is no charge to use the trails. In winter romp through the snow-covered fields and forests. Programs range from mammal tracking to snowshoe making. Full-moon snowshoeing, a maple-sugaring celebration, and horse-drawn sleigh rides are also offered during winter. Or spend a day indoors learning how to make a packbasket while other family members head out on the trails. Nature displays can be found at the visitor center and in the farmhouse on Old Town Road.

It is fairly easy to get around the property. Its signs are easy to read though they do not have distances on them. The trails are not marked with occasional blazes or markers as in national forests, which is a slight drawback. This might prove worrisome to those new to the outdoor experience. If that is the case, just ask at the visitor center for the trails that have seen recent usage. These packed paths will be easy to follow.

We've put together an interesting 3.5-mile loop to give visitors a taste of what is on the property. But feel free to explore a side trail, particularly after a fresh snow.

Directions at a glance

0.0 Leave the visitor center via Old Town Road. Follow Old Town Road 1.5 miles. Look for sign to Birch Pond.

1.5 Turn right at sign to Birch Pond. Continue uphill from Birch Pond to Clark's Clearing Trail via Schnenk Road.

2.0 Cabin marks the intersection with Antone Road. Turn left on Antone Road.

2.7 Bear left on Old Town Road and follow it 0.8 mile back to the visitor center.

Old Town Road is a wide, unplowed road that goes through the heart of the property. Remember this is a working farm. Wide, thick wheels from farm equipment provide a country track for skiers. Or you can ski or snowshoe on the bank of snow left between the tires. Leave the visitor center on Old Town Road as it opens up to a stunning vista of farm, hills, and horses. Look for the tepee off to the left. A cabin appears on the right, and the farmhouse appears more like a castle in the outdoor beauty. Pass by the horses, then turn right with Old Town Road as it climbs steadily along. Enjoy the stunning views of the Taconics. On both sides several trails leave Old Town Road. At the height of land, a road to a lodge diverges left and one to Mount Antone leaves right. Continue straight on Old Town. Admire the stands of spruce and hilltops. Old Town Road descends quickly here as it passes along a maple grove. In late February the sugar maple trees are tapped with a line that stretches from tree to tree. Near the 1.5-mile mark, a sign points to Birch Pond. As an excellent diversion you can return along the same way. To make the loop turn right by the sign to Birch Pond, a small pond set among the hills.

Clark's Clearing Trail ascends the forested hill. There won't be a sign yet. There is one for Schenk Road, which leads to Clark's Clearing Trail. The trail has a few steep grades as it climbs upward along the flanks of Mount Antone. The trail reaches a small cabin called the Clark's Clearing Cabin. (In the cabin are a bunk bed, table, and woodstove.) A number of trails intersect here. Just turn right at the cabin for Antone Road and head

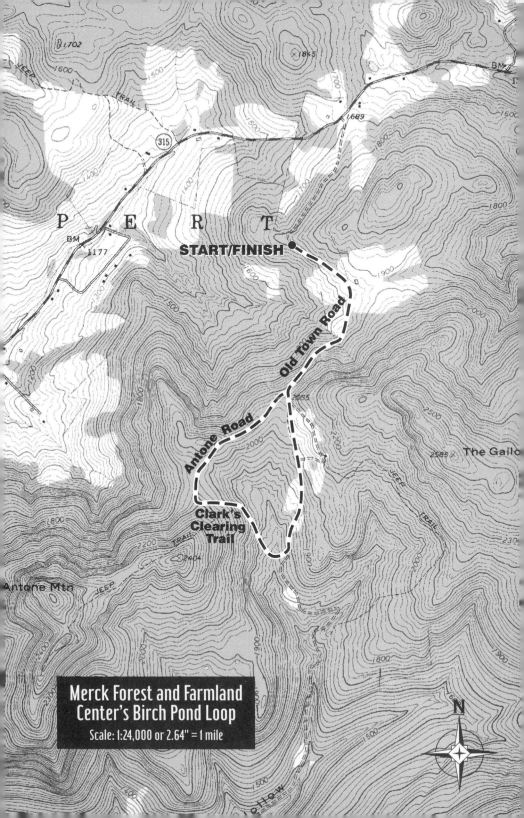

START/FINISH

Old Town Road

Antone Road

Clark's
Clearing
Trail

P E R T

Merck Forest and Farmland
Center's Birch Pond Loop
Scale: 1:24,000 or 2.64" = 1 mile

N

The beauty of Merck Forest and Farmland Center is reflected on the Old Town Road.

to the clearing for a beautiful vista. Antone Road slopes downward to join up with Old Town Road. Bear left on Old Town Road (this junction should look familiar) and follow it back down to the visitor center.

How to get there

From Manchester travel on West Road 3.5 miles. Turn left on Route 30 north to Dorset. Travel 5.5 miles and turn left on Route 315. Go about 3.0 miles and turn left at the Merck Forest and Farmland Center in Rupert.

Little Michigan/Stone Place Trails Loop

Landgrove, Vermont

Type of trail:	▬▬ ⬤
Also used by:	Small portion by snowmobilers
Distance:	4.0 miles
Terrain:	Hilly
Trail difficulty:	More and most difficult
Surface quality:	Ungroomed, skier tracked
Food and facilities:	There are no facilities available on this loop. Cross-country ski and snowshoe rentals and lessons can be had at the Landgrove Inn, Little Michigan Road, Landgrove (802–824–6673), a short distance from the trailhead. The West River Nordic Ski Club's Trail Network with a few miles of groomed trails is at the inn. It has some beginners' trails. Donations are accepted. For groceries try the Mountain Marketplace shopping center at the junctions of Routes 11 and 100 in Londonderry. Jake's Cafe (802–824–6614) is there for a post-ski meal. The Landgrove Inn serves dinner Thursday through Sunday evenings.
Phone numbers:	Green Mountain National Forest Manchester Ranger District, (802) 362–2307; Mountain Valley Trails Association, (802) 824–4166.

Skiers and snowshoers looking for a 10-mile network of challenging trails in southern Vermont should head to the rural village of Landgrove and the Mountain Valley Trails Association area in the Green Mountain National Forest. The farms, brooks, horses, old cemeteries, and New England quaintness is a most pleasant diversion from the intermediate and advanced trails on the surrounding hills.

Located in the national forest, the trails are ungroomed and open to the public at no charge. (There are a few loop options available, like the 7.0-mile Little Michigan Loop.) They are well marked with blue diamonds and signs. Here, we go a little more than half that distance in a hillside workout that also encompasses Vermont's legendary Catamount Cross-Country Ski Trail.

Snowmobilers like this part of the world, too. You share the trail, Forest Road 10, with them for only a short distance.

The Little Michigan Loop trailhead is on Forest Road 10. Ski on the wide forest road beyond the sign board to a sign that points left to the Catamount Ski Trail/Utley Brook Trail. A black diamond ski sign indicates that the route is most difficult. That may well be because of the climb involved. In reality, initially, the Utley Brook Trail wiggles through the evergreens like a playful puppy. But that puppy grows up rather quickly and takes a snap at you from time to time with a few heart-stopping pitches and narrow slots through the trees.

Remember that some of the trails in the Green Mountain National Forest go through periods of active timber operations. A portion of the Utley Brook Trail was being harvested in the early winter of 1998. The trail widens considerably as it passes through the harvest area up along the side of a hill. The reward is a hoot of a ski down to the junction with the Little Michigan Trail. Turn left on Little Michigan for a short and gentle climb to the junction with the Stone Place Trail. Skiers and shoers looking for the 7.0-mile loop should continue on the Little Michigan Trail until reaching the Jones Brook Trail and return to the parking area.

Turn left for the Stone Place Trail and descend. The trail includes a small section that is a wide, flat unplowed country road. Ski down and at the junction with the road, turn right. Enjoy the flatness and brightness. At about 0.2 mile a bridge off to the left crosses picturesque Griffith Brook. Cross the railed bridge as the trail continues a moderate climb. The trail plays with the sun: Sometimes it is sunny in spots; other times, shaded by the forest pines.

Directions at a glance

0.0 From the Little Michigan trailhead on Forest Road 10, ski down the road a few yards until reaching a sign for the Catamount Cross-Country Ski Trail. Turn left. This is the Utley Brook Trail.

1.2 Turn left on Little Michigan Trail.

1.4 Turn left on Stone Place Trail.

1.5 Turn right on the Stone Place Trail.

1.7 Turn left over the bridge on the Stone Place Trail.

2.4 Turn left on the Jones Brook Trail.

3.7 Turn left on groomed trail, part of West River Nordic Ski Club system. It is unsigned. Continue straight for a few yards. Trail will bear right. Ski down hill to the left into meadow and continue bearing left to ski club parking area on Little Michigan Road. Turn left out of parking area on Little Michigan Road.

3.8 Turn right on Forest Road 10.

4.0 To the left is the Little Michigan trailhead.

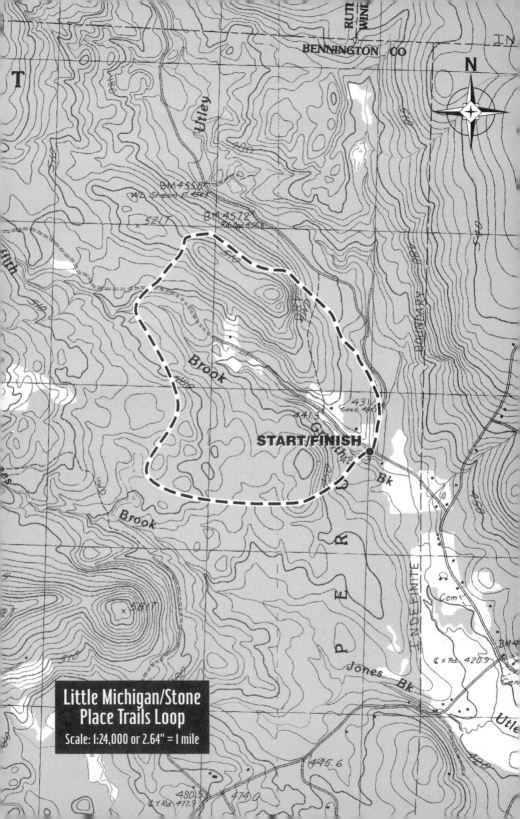

START/FINISH

Little Michigan/Stone
Place Trails Loop
Scale: 1:24,000 or 2.64" = 1 mile

A junction marks a left turn onto the Jones Brook Trail. Like a winter desert, small young growths poke through the snow. The distant alpine slopes of Bromley act as a backdrop. The Jones Brook Trail rolls downward before darting left back into the woods. Over the next 1.0 mile, the trail has several rolling hills, including an exhilarating sweeping hairpin curve.

The Jones Brook Trail comes to a T junction with a groomed trail, part of the West River Nordic Ski Club's Trail Network. Turn left on the velvetlike thoroughfare and ski a few yards. The trail will bear right. Instead, shoot down that hill to the left and into the meadow. Continue bearing left until you reach the ski club's parking area.

From here either ski back to the car by turning left on Little Michigan Road and right on FR 10, or take off the skis, watch the horses, and stretch those legs before walking back to the car.

How to get there

From the junction of Routes 100 and 11 in Londonderry, travel on Route 11 west. Proceed 0.5 mile and turn right on Landgrove Road. Follow Landgrove Road 4.2 miles and turn left on Little Michigan Road. One-half mile later, turn right on Forest Road 10. A sign will point to Danby. The trailhead is 0.2 mile down on the left, but parking is not allowed there because it is a plow turnaround point. Park along the road but not in front of the no parking signs.

Not exactly Detroit, as a skier digs into his backpack along the Little Michigan Trail.

Grout Pond Loop Trail
Stratton, Vermont

Type of trail:	▬▬▬▬ ⬬
Also used by:	Portion by snowmobilers
Distance:	4.8 miles
Terrain:	Flat to rolling
Trail difficulty:	Easiest
Surface quality:	Ungroomed, but portions groomed by snowmobilers and skier tracked
Food and facilities:	There is no water. Toilets are available along the way, as is a warming cabin and lean-to shelters. There are general stores in nearby West Wardsboro and Wardsboro. If you are coming from the Stratton Mountain Ski Area, rentals are available there, as are convenience stores. After the ski there is Norm's on Routes 30/100 in Jamaica for Italian (802–874–7004).
Phone numbers:	Manchester Ranger District of the Green Mountain National Forest, (802) 362–2307.

The loop around Grout Pond is like a pizza with your favorite toppings. Throw in a tiny slice of Vermont's state-long cross-country trail, add a handful of small rolling dips, toss in views of alpine slopes, sprinkle on some pristine pond vistas, and shake on a dab or two of warmth at a trailside cabin and shelter, and you've got a tasty adventure.

The Grout Pond Recreation Area south of Stratton Mountain has about 12 miles of interconnected trails in the Green Mountain National Forest. The network offers many opportunities for skiers and snowshoers along the easy and more difficult well-marked trails that circumnavigate the pond and lead to the shores of Somerset Reservoir. A small portion of the loop utilizes the Catamount Ski Trail, a 300-mile-long trail that runs from the Massachusetts border to Canada,
roughly paralleling the Long Trail. Long Trail is maintained by the Catamount Trail Association, founded in 1985.

Directions at a glance

0.0 Leave the parking area, cross the road, and travel on FR 262, also known as the Catamount Ski Trail.

0.5 Turn left on the East Trail.

0.6 Turn right on the East Trail.

1.3 Turn left on the Pond Trail.

3.6 Turn right on FR 262 and travel 1.2 miles back to the parking area.

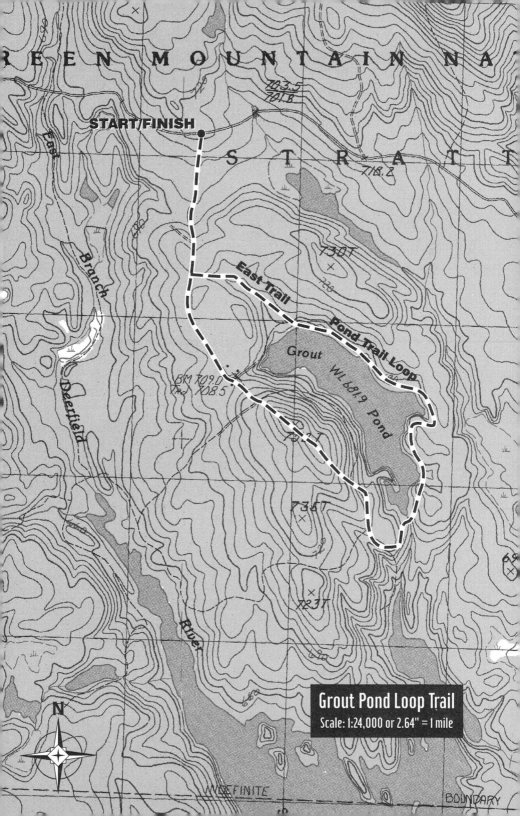

Not only is the Grout Pond area ski country, there are also snowmobile trails in the neighborhood. Skier, snowshoers, and snowmobilers share the same parking area and about a 1.0-mile section of the loop. The snowmobile trails, blazed in orange, are maintained by the Vermont Association of Snow Travelers.

A skier pauses on the Pond Trail around Grout Pond in Vermont to reflect upon the distant ski slopes.

Winter campers, particularly those on snowshoes, can use this loop as an overnight excursion. Grout Pond is home to three lean-tos. One lean-to is accessible via the Pond Trail and provides views of Mount Snow's ski trails.

The loop begins along Forest Road 262, also part of the Catamount Ski Trail. The superwide trail is also used by snowmobiles, which pack it. Cruise down and roll up to a junction with the East Trail and turn left. Blue diamonds show you the way. The Forest Service has excellent signs and also uses letters that correspond with its map to record distances. The trail narrows in the woods. It is here that the fun really begins—it is like riding a camel with a never-ending assortment of humps. The East Trail gives way to the Pond Trail, which circles Grout Pond. The oblong pond is to your right. Soon a lean-to will appear just off the trail on the left. Many of the views of the pond are through trees, but on occasion the vistas open up, offering a photo opportunity.

Pond Trail rounds the southeastern shore of Grout Pond and soon parts company with it. Cross over a bridge with handrails and stay with the Pond Trail as it becomes part of the Catamount again. The trail ascends along the western side of the pond, and there are wonderful respites thrown in for good measure: The Pond Trail will come out by a cabin with a toilet next to it. Head to the table and have some lunch. Continue past the cabin to another that has seen better days.

The Pond Trail leads you to FR 262 again when you bear to the right. The wide snowmobile trail returns. Follow along. A wildlife viewing area will appear on the left. Moose tracks and game birds have been spotted in the recreation area. The familiar East Trail will enter right. Ski the final half mile back to the parking area.

How to get there

From Waldeboro (Route 100) turn right on the Arlington–West Wardsboro Road (sign points to Stratton.) Travel through West Wardsboro and the small town of Stratton 6.5 miles to the Grout Mountain Recreation Parking Area on the right. Along the way the road becomes Kelley Stand Road (Forest Route 6).

Big Bear Loop

Grafton Ponds Nordic Ski Center, Grafton, Vermont

Type of trail:	▰▰ ◁ ▱
Distance:	4.7 miles
Terrain:	Flat to hilly
Trail difficulty:	More difficult
Surface quality:	Groomed, skate lane, double tracked
Food and facilities:	Rentals (skis and snowshoes), lessons, retail shop, snowmaking, skating, snow tubing, wax room, and cold and hot snacks are available at the touring center. There is a trail fee. For dinner try The Old Tavern (800–843–1801) just down Townsend Road in Grafton. The Big Bear Cabin on this loop is an ideal lunch and warming up spot. The Grafton Village Store in the town center is handy for quick items and sandwiches. The Grafton Village Cheese Company (next to the ski center) provides samples of its six types of cheddar (and it is possible to ski from the ski center to the cheese company).
Phone numbers:	The Grafton Ponds Nordic Ski Center, (802) 843–2400.

Time appears to stand still in the quaint community of Grafton, Vermont. Nestled in southeastern Vermont among farms and forest, the little town of 600 once subsisted on farming and logging. But the Great Depression in the 1930s put the economy on the skids. Enter the Windham Foundation, a philanthropic nonprofit historic preservation organization. It bought up much of the land and many of the buildings in the valley and has worked to revitalize the community, which is now home to a thriving, quaint inn, cheese factory, and 20 miles of skate-friendly cross-country ski trails.

The trails at Grafton, including about 10 miles just for snowshoeing, are found in a valley between Grafton and Townsend at the base of Big

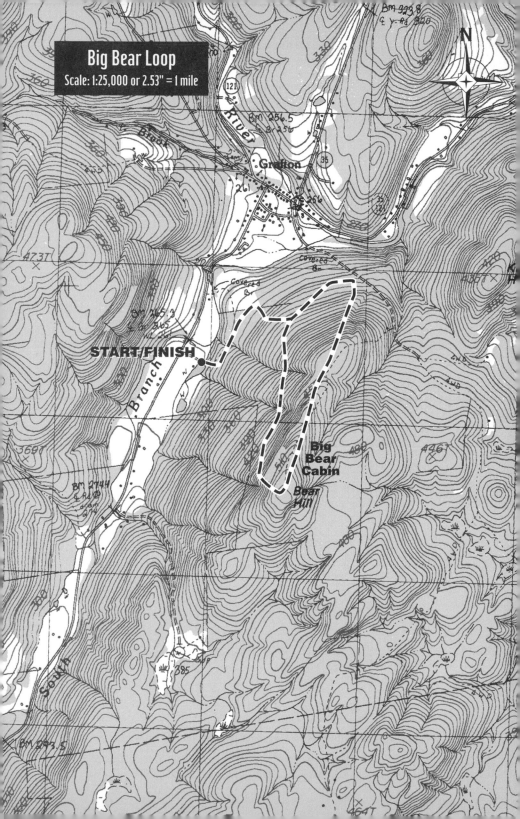

Bear Mountain. The gentle ridge lines running through the hardwood and softwood forests are gateways to long, extended views down on the village with its two pert, white church steeples and neighboring hills.

The rustic Nordic center has both a fireplace and woodstove for those cold, winter days, while the Big Bear Cabin, near the midpoint on this loop, is kept warm on the weekends by its own woodstove.

Interestingly Grafton has no trails that are graded most difficult. And though the Big Bear Loop is labeled more difficult, it is only because of a couple of steep, short pitches that climb up to the cabin. Also the trails at Grafton are extremely wide, making it a winter playground for skate skiers. During this tour skiers need not worry about skiers barreling down as they climb. The loop runs one way.

Begin outside the touring center on Main Trail in front of the warm-up field. The network is well marked with signs naming the trail. Ski or snowshoe past the frozen ponds and bear left as the trail gently ascends through the birch trees. Be sure to stop at the Village Overlook for a soothing look out at the snow-covered meadows, sleepy village with woodstoves ablaze, and Spring Hill in the background. Main Trail gives way to the right to Little Bear, which has a bit more bite. Spot fox, turkey, deer, and even occasional bear tracks (not surprisingly) on the trails. Keep an eye out for them on the snow, and the hawks that circle overhead. Little Bear ascends to a winding Big Bear during the 600-foot climb to the highest point on the trail. Near the 2-mile mark, the small Big Bear Cabin is a welcome sight. Through the birch, spruce, and pine forest, look across to Burt Hill and try to spot Target Rock. It is said the rock was used as a marker by a man who lived in the area in the 1940s and 1950s. He flew airplanes, and the rock was like a flight tower, marking a spot close to where he could land his aircraft on a grassy runway.

The time has come for a nearly 2-mile downhill run on Big and Little Bear Trails. Leave the warmth of the cabin and continue on Big Bear for a long, easy, and winding ride. About three-quarters of a mile from the cabin, try and take a rest at the Grafton Overlook, which provides another cozy village scene. Signs point to the touring center and are easy to follow back as Big Bear weaves into Little Bear and back to Main Trail.

Directions at a glance

0.0 Leave the touring center on Main Trail and bear left about 100 yards.

0.5 Turn right on Little Bear.

1.5 Bear left on Big Bear.

4.0 Bear right on Little Bear.

4.2 Bear right on Main Trail and ski 0.5 mile back to the touring center.

How to get there

From I–91 take exit 7 and follow Route 11 west some 12.3 miles. Turn left in Chester on Route 35 south. Travel on Route 35 south for some 7.4 miles. Turn right on Main Street (Route 121) in Grafton. Follow it for a few hundred yards and turn left on Townsend Road. Grafton Ponds is down the road about three-quarters of a mile.

Mount Olga Trail

Molly Stark State Park, Wilmington, Vermont

Type of trail:	(icon)
Also used by:	Hikers
Distance:	2.3 miles
Terrain:	Flat to hilly
Trail difficulty:	Easiest
Surface quality:	Ungroomed
Food and facilities:	There are no facilities. A fire tower is near the loop's mid-point. Wilmington has supplies. There is a Grand Union on Route 9. Try Sonny's Cup and Saucer on Route 100 next to a general store for after the snowshoe, (802) 464–5813.
Phone numbers:	Winter phone number for Molly Stark State Park, (802) 886–2434.

Why climb a mountain? "Because it's there" is the famous answer. "Because of the views" is the answer for climbing the small, but fire-tower-view heavy 2,415-foot Mount Olga in southern Vermont's Molly Stark State Park. To be fair the summit on Mount Olga is actually quite cluttered. There are a few wooden maintenance shacks for the antenna perched atop the mountain. While standing on the summit, you can't see a thing.

So, what do you do?

Take off those snowshoes and start climbing the steps of the fire tower. From the enclosed tower the spectacular 360-degree panorama takes in portions of three states—southern Vermont, northern Massachusetts, and southwestern New Hampshire. Valley floors give way to alpine slopes. Evergreens frame each picture from the window panes in the fire tower.

The loop trail up and down Mount Olga is fairly easy, winding through the evergreens to the summit. There are a few moderate pitches along the way, but they are quickly and easily conquered.

The Mount Olga Trail is blazed in blue. Skiing it is not recommended.

The park road into the state park is the gateway to the trail. Snowshoe past the closed gate along the park road. A rushing brook parallels the snow-covered road. The brown park headquarters building is at the top of the gentle incline. The trailhead is across the building on the left side of the park road by the brook.

The trail immediately crosses a wooden bridge over the little stream and starts a gradual climb through the forest. The trail passes through stone walls twice, though they may be obscured, depending on how much snow has fallen. Soon enough you reach a junction. Here the Mount Olga Trail continues right back to the campground. Remember this junction and head up another 0.1 mile to the summit.

Climb the fire tower and drink in the views.

Descend the summit the same way and be sure to follow the Mount Olga Trail to the left back to the campground. The trail descends gradually along a stone wall. There are a couple of small stream crossings along the descent. Use the rocks to negotiate the trickling waters.

The trail heads to the campground and follows the park road back to park headquarters. As a point of reference, the first lean-to passed is named "Poplar" and the second is named "Spruce." Turn left on the park road through the campground. It will sweep right and pass the familiar park headquarters building. Pass headquarters and turn left back down to the gate.

Directions at a glance

0.0 Go around the gate at the entrance of the Molly Stark State Park and proceed along the park road.

0.2 Turn left by the sign for the Olga Mountain Trail, which is across from brown park headquarters in the park/campground, and follow it 0.8 mile to the junction.

0.9 Head straight at the signed junction to the summit. From the summit return back to junction and turn left by the sign on Olga Mountain Trail, which is a 0.9-mile path to the campground.

2.0 Turn left on the park road and follow it back to park headquarters.

2.2 Turn left on park road by park headquarters and follow it 0.2 mile back to the gate by the park entrance.

A stream rushes below the trails of Mount Olga.

How to get there

From Wilmington travel east on Route 9 about 3.4 miles. The entrance to the Molly Stark State Park is at 3.5 miles, but the entrance is not plowed. So, at the 3.4-mile mark from Wilmington, turn left on Sparrow Lane and follow it to the plowed turnaround. Park there so as not to interfere with traffic. The entrance to the park is across Route 9.

Old Railroad Bed/West River Trail

Jamaica State Park, Jamaica, Vermont

Type of trail:	▬▬ ⬤
Also used by:	Winter hikers
Distance:	2.3 miles one way, 4.6 miles round-trip (optional side trip)
Terrain:	Flat
Trail difficulty:	Easiest
Surface quality:	Ungroomed
Food and facilities:	There are no facilities. The Jamaica Corner Store on Route 30 has food and drink.
Phone numbers:	Winter phone number for Jamaica State Park, (802) 886–2434.

Though the railroad that once ran alongside the white-capped West River was called "36 miles of trouble," the flat and scenic section that you access through Jamaica State Park is anything but trouble. The West River Railroad chugged along between Brattleboro and Londonderry from 1879 to 1935. But the railroad had its problems. Money was tight, so it was built with cheap materials. Throw in steep terrain, sharp corners, foul weather, and cold, snowy Vermont winters and that adds up to trouble. A devastating flood in 1927 nearly wiped out the tracks, so in 1939 the tracks were torn up. The rail bed remains as the park's Old Railroad Bed/West River Trail. It is a 2-mile-wide stretch with nine nature stops filled with historical and ecological information about the area, running alongside the dark, rushing river waters, strewn with snow-capped rocks in a narrow gorge.

Directions at a glance

0.0 Leave the plowed out parking area of Jamaica State Park by going around the gate and through the campground, which parallels the West River.

0.3 Leave the day camping area by a sign that points to a number of trails: Railroad Bed Trail, Bald Mountain Dam, Overlook Trail, Hamilton Falls. Go straight.

2.2 Turn right at Hamilton Falls Trail for optional out-and-back moderate snowshoe to falls.

2.3 Reach the end of the trail by station 9 and the bench. Return at the same way.

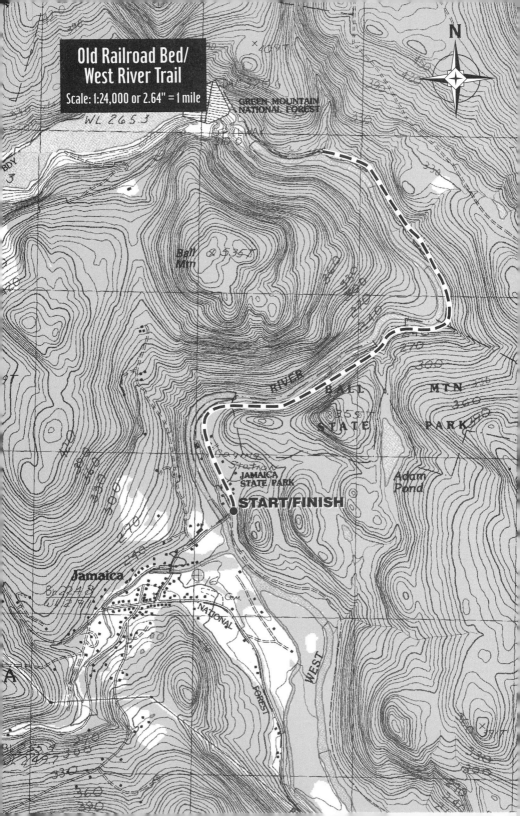

Pass through the dormant campground to the sleeping nature center and then the swimming area in the river. Soon the nature boxes will appear.

Ferns and carpetlike green moss grow from the huge boulders, signs of ancient glacial activity. Birches, hemlocks, spruce, ash, maple, and others fill the spectacular gorge. The interpretive signs in the boxes are an outdoor treasure trove of information. On top, each box gives a story about a particular subject. Open them up and inside is a little science lesson about the wildlife and flora and fauna that inhabit the area. There are also mileage markers that tell you the distance from the dormant nature center. Benches and picnic tables are scattered along the trails as well.

There is a sense of nature's circle of life along this trail. As winter turns to spring, the snow melts and flows into the West River, feeding it. Its churning waters then attract kayakers. Even before the Ball Mountain Dam was built upriver, white-water enthusiasts came here to test their skills. Now they come in April and September to challenge the roiling waters.

The water is your constant companion during this flat adventure. The easiness of the trail, rest stops, and nature signs make this trip ideal for families with children. They will also enjoy the mini-waterfalls along the way.

If you are here in late winter as spring approaches, you'll hear the waters' thunderous tone. For a most dramatic vantage point, go where the trail and river bend hard to the left, a point called the "Ox bow," between stations five and six. At station six learn about this U-shaped bend created by erosion.

It should be noted that the West River Trail accesses the Hamilton Falls Trail, which leads to one of the most beautiful waterfalls in the state. Hamilton Falls drops 125 feet and becomes a frozen masterpiece in winter. The trail to the falls is a long, moderate 1.2-mile climb along an old road high atop Cobb Brook. It is for better snowshoers. The trail to the falls leaves right at 1.9 miles. The falls have claimed at least ten lives in recent years, a nearby sign notes.

Station nine marks the end of this West River Trail adventure. The bench is a fine place to watch Cobb Brook flow into the West River by the old stone bridge abutments. Rest up and return along the same route.

How to get there
From Jamaica turn on Depot Street and follow it 0.5 mile past the school, over the bridge, and to the small plowed-out parking area on the left.

new hampshire

B&M Trail

Bretton Woods, New Hampshire

Type of trail:	▬▬ ＜ ⬭
Distance:	7.5 miles; a shorter 5.0-mile loop option
Terrain:	Flat, gradual incline, downhill
Trail difficulty:	Easiest to more difficult
Surface quality:	Groomed, single tracked, double tracked
Food and facilities:	Cross-country and snowshoe rentals, instruction, a cafeteria, wax room, and rest rooms are available at the Bretton Woods Cross-Country Ski Center; trail passes are also sold in the center. No food, rest rooms, or water are available during the tour. There is an unheated shelter with an outdoor fire pit about midway. Nearby Fabyan's Station (603–278–2222), a renovated train station, serves lunch and dinner.
Phone numbers:	Toll-free number for Bretton Woods, (800) 232–2972; direct line to the cross-country center, (603) 278–3322.

With an impressive backdrop of the rugged snow-capped Presidential Range and the beauty of the red-roofed Mount Washington Hotel, the Bretton Woods Cross-Country Ski Center serves up more than 60 miles of trails for skiers and snowshoers.

Some 80 percent of visitors stick to the Ammonoosuc Trail System with its network of wide, flat beginner trails and friendly intermediate routes. This loop utilizes that system. The Deception System has more varied and challenging terrain, including a trail that traverses Mount Deception. The Stickney System is the lift-served network found by the slopes of the downhill ski area, which includes the curves of Mountain Road. The Perimeter Trail, double tracked with a skate lane in the middle, circumnavigates a golf course, offering a flat, open route with majestic views of the mountains and hotel. (The hotel, complete with a railed veranda sweeping around its white face, opened in 1902 and is now a National Historic Landmark.)

The Ammonoosuc flows from Mount Washington, the Northeast's highest peak at 6,288 feet, and parallels the B&M Trail for a spell. The B&M trail follows an abandoned railroad bed—the line once used to access the Cog Railroad—which goes to the top of Mount Washington. The B&M is primarily a straight shot through the woods, with a few rollers near the end.

B & M Trail

Scale: 1:25,000 or 2.53" = 1 mile

The historic Mount Washington Hotel is set in front of a Presidential backdrop on the Bretton Woods Cross-Country network.

The B&M enters the woods. It is narrow and tunnel-like, lined with firs. Look down on the pools of water during the gentle ascent. Though there is a skate lane, skate skiers might prefer the wider Bridle Path that parallels the B&M and later rejoins it. The Bridle Path dates back to the 1800s when it was used as a horse path. A short side trip well worth taking is the 50-foot jaunt off the B&M to Upper Falls. Here a bridge and gorge team up for a glorious view of the summit of Mount Monroe.

About midway through the loop, you'll find an unheated shelter, an enjoyable spot for a snack. The Porcupine Lane is more playful and has a few interesting curves. About 0.5 mile into Porcupine Lane, the route begins its descent (some 500 feet had been gained in elevation during this tour). Round a bend on Porcupine and come to a junction with Sebosis, a trail labeled more difficult, no doubt due to its winding, snakelike downhill. Sebosis is a blast as it winds its way back down to the flats. Firs and birches line the trail. Several wide and easy bridge crossings over brooks are part of the descent. You leave the sheltered

Directions at a glance

0.0 Leave the cross-country ski center via the Perimeter Trail. There is one section where skiers should take off skis before crossing a hotel road.

0.5 Follow the Perimeter Trail. It will merge with a connector trail that points the way to the B&M Trail.

1.0 Bear left on the B&M Trail and follow it for some 3.0 miles.

4.0 Turn right on Porcupine Lane.

4.7 Turn right on Sebosis.

6.7 Stay straight on the Perimeter Trail leading back to the cross-country center. There is one section where skiers should take off skis before crossing the hotel road.

Alternative loop

0.0 Leave the cross-country ski center via the Perimeter Trail. Take off skis when crossing the hotel road.

0.5 Turn left on Perimeter and cross Stone Pillar Bridge.

0.8 Turn right on Bridle Path, which merges (after 1.3 miles) with B&M Trail.

2.3 Turn left to Upper Falls Bridge. Return back to B&M Trail.

2.5 Turn right on B&M Trail.

4.0 Turn right on Perimeter, which leads to the hotel.

woods behind where Sebosis rejoins the flats of the Perimeter Trail where the Presidentials stand guard over the rear of the hotel. You can take a shorter, equally scenic tour of about 5.0 miles by combining a loop of the the Bridle Path and B&M. This loop shaves about 2.5 miles from the aforementioned trip.

How to get there

From I–93 north take exit 35 (Route 3 north) to Route 302 east. The cross-country ski center is based near the Mount Washington Hotel.

Canal Trail
The Balsams, Dixville Notch, New Hampshire

Type of trail:	▬▬ ⫷
Distance:	7.4 miles; option exists for additional 2.0-mile loop
Terrain:	Gradual incline, flat, followed by welcomed downhill
Trail difficulty:	Easiest
Surface quality:	Groomed, rolled, single tracked, double tracked
Food and facilities:	A trail fee is required for access to The Balsams' cross-country trails (not for registered hotel guests). Cross-country skis and snowshoes are available for rent inside the hotel; instruction and a wax room are also available. Snowshoeing is not allowed on the cross-country trails, but is allowed on a network of snowshoe-only trails. A warming hut is an ideal lunch spot. Toilet facilities are located outside the warming hut. Food and water are not available during the ski, so bring your own. For post-ski sustenance there is the elegant Balsams. Or try burgers at Errol Restaurant and Pub some 9 miles away (603–482–3852).
Phone numbers:	Three telephone numbers for The Balsams: toll-free in the continental U.S. and Canada, (800) 255–0600; toll-free in New Hampshire, (800) 255–0800; also a general business number, (603) 255–3400.

The 50 miles of numbered cross-country trails at The Balsams Grand Resort Hotel in northern New Hampshire are set amidst the majesty of the dramatic cliffs of Dixville Notch and the grandeur of the resort itself. The northeast quadrant of the network is home to miles of groomed beginner trails, centering on the remote Mud Pond as a destination. Though this tour gains 500 feet in elevation, the gentle climb along the tree-guarded trails is but a memory after a rest stop in a toasty warming hut along the pond's frozen shores.

History and nature hold a friendly competition for the skier's attention because the tour is filled with both. The well-protected Golf Course Road Trail (no. 0) makes a slow ascent through sugar maples, passing the Two Town Pond. The pond used to be part of the irrigation system for local farms. Beavers prefer it now. You also have distant views of Canada's Mount Hereford and Vermont's Mount Monadnock. The Moose Pond Trail, which follows Moose Brook, traverses the northern base of Mount Abenaki, where rare peregrine falcons soar in March.

Directions at a glance

0.0 Begin at the Golf Course Road trailhead and ski the well-signed Golf Course Road Trail (no. 0).

1.5 Turn right on Moose Pond Trail (no. 12)—there is a sign—and ski it for 1.0 mile.

2.5 Turn right at the sign for the Tunnel Trail (no. 10) and ski about .25 mile to the top of the hill.

2.75 At the top of the hill, make a sharp left on the Valley Trail (no. 14) and ski down about 30 yards to the Canal Trail (no. 8).

2.75 Turn right on the Canal Trail (no. 8) and follow it 1.2 miles to Mud Pond.

3.9 At Mud Pond turn left on the Mud Pond Loop Trail (no. 24) and ski about 60 yards to the warming hut. As an option skiers might want to ski the entire Mud Pond Loop Trail (no. 24) clockwise. The 2.0-mile loop offers fine sporadic views of the pond.

3.9 From the Mud Pond Loop Trail, turn left on Moose Pond Trail (no. 12) and ski it about 2.0 miles, staying straight at the various intersections along the way.

5.9 Turn left on the Golf Course Road Trail (no. 0) and ski it approximately 1.5 miles back to the trailhead where the loop began.

The Tunnel and Valley Trails, the short intermediate bursts on the loop, are the gateways to a most pleasant ski—the Canal Trail. Perhaps it should be called "Christmas Tree Lane" becuase it winds narrowly through a forest of balsam firs. The trail, which is rolled, runs parallel to a hand-cut canal that once brought water from Mud Pond to the hotel. The Canal Trail is a rare treat, giving the illusion of traversing a ridge. Relax a bit at the heated warming hut on the southwest corner of Mud Pond. Plump Canada jays may coax you out of a snack. The option exists here for a 2-mile easy ski around the pond. Keep eyes alert for moose tracks if you go. The views on the northern edge of the pond are worth the trip.

The elevation at Mud Pond is 2,322 feet, a gain of nearly 500 feet in altitude from the hotel, set at 1,846 feet. Now comes time for the reward. Revisit the Moose Pond Trail. The ski begins as a downhill. But don't put all of that energy away. There are a few little pulls to negotiate. After the

A snowshoer takes in the views on the Cliffside Trail, one of many snowshoe-only trails at The Balsams resort.

downhill enjoy a cruise along the wide path as Moose Pond yields back to the Golf Course Road Trail. Gaze into the distance of Dixville Notch. It is along this trail that skiers can see why a mountain pass is called a "notch" in New Hampshire. The V-shaped cut is obvious, as are the steep sides of the narrow notch.

How to get there

From Boston head north on I–93 past Franconia Notch to exit 35, then Route 3 to Colebrook, and east on Route 26 to Dixville Notch (210 miles). Park in The Balsams' lot. Trail passes are sold inside the hotel at the cross-country center. It is then a five-minute walk to the well-signed trailhead.

Hayes Copp Ski Trail/Leavitt's Link
Gorham, New Hampshire

Type of trail:	▬▬ ⬭
Also used by:	Hikers
Distance:	5.0 miles
Terrain:	Flat to rolling
Trail difficulty:	Easiest, more difficult
Surface quality:	Ungroomed, skier tracked
Food and facilities:	Public telephones and toilets are available near the trailhead. Winter camping is open at Barnes Field, also near the trailhead. Vehicles must display the White Mountain National Forest user fee sticker required to park. After the ski, Gorham has a couple of Chinese restaurants with all-you-can-eat buffets, like the Golden Maple (603–466–2766). Gorham also has a few shops for ski and snowshoe rentals.
Phone numbers:	White Mountain National Forest's Androscoggin Ranger Station for skiing conditions, (603) 466–2713; the station, just north of the trailhead on Route 16, has a wealth of information and interpretive displays. New Hampshire State Police, (800) 525–5555.

Hayes and Dolly Copp were a couple of tourism pioneers, though at the time they probably didn't know it. In 1827 Hayes traveled up through Pinkham Notch, spotted a place along the flats of the Peabody River that he thought might make a good farm, and cleared the land. Fours years later, he had a wife named Dolly, a one-room cabin, and some crops. The next thing you know they have four children and a farm and have started to greet visitors traveling to Mount Washington. Now a ski trail is named after Hayes, and a campground after Dolly.

Much of the Hayes Copp Cross-Country Ski Trail is on logging roads, a beginner's delight. Though there is an 8.0-mile network that borders the Great Gulf Wilderness, the 5.0-mile loop is a fine outing for many a skier and snowshoer. The east side of the loop, including Leavitt's Link, is largely flat and inviting. Then it heads away from the hibernating Dolly Copp Campground and into the woods to climb oh-so-gently on the Great Gulf Link with an occasional herringbone along the Peabody River. This section is quiet and peaceful, unless a large truck happens to be huffing by on Route 16, and the river's frozen waters are a pleasure to the eye. But we are getting ahead of ourselves.

The tour begins from the well-marked Dolly Copp Campground. Sign in before the tour! Then ski—or snowshoe—through the sleeping campground with snow-covered picnic tables, taps, garbage bins, and fields. Initally, the trail along the road is flat and very wide. It is marked with plastic blue squares. The outline of the Carter Range into Pinkham Notch is quite obvious to your left. Look for the Imp Profile, a cliff on a west spur of North Carter. At about the 0.5-mile mark you cross the Culhane Brook via a bridge. On the right sharp eyes can spot the cap of 4,890-foot Mount Madison. Ski right by the Daniel Webster Scout Trail, which leads to that very mountain.

There is an option shortly after the Webster Trail. Though it is not obvious, a ski trail bears to the right. Don't fret if you miss it. Stay on the campground road until it ends at the Great Gulf Link. Now, the trail enters the woods and narrows, riding along the banks of the Peabody. The ski tracks may be finished for a while as hikers and snowshoers share this corridor. Perhaps a snowshoe hare will dart by. In the woods occasional signs with Nordic skiers are posted on trees. The trail follows the river and climbs a tad more steeply as it continues along the Great Gulf Trail, which it diverges from at Leavitt's Link. Beginners might consider heading back along the same way because Leavitt's Link rolls more and has some climbs. A sign at this junction outlines all the trails and distances. Turn right and climb up to a clearing on Leavitt's Link. Here are panoramic views of the Carter Range and glimpses of the Presidentials. This is a fine spot for a snack. Look for a couple of stumps that are usually there by a firepit. Get refueled because the trail will roll. There will be more than twenty bridge crossings after this point. Just after a large, fresh snowfall, you'll hardly notice the small bridges. But if conditions are icy, steel nerves help. Leavitt's Link is hilly and seems to go along the outline of the Carter Range. The trail is very easy to follow and leads back to the parking lot. Ski or snowshoe it for about 1.5 miles before the Hayes Copp Trail returns from the left. One-half mile later, after crossing a bridge over the Culhane Brook, look closely to the right for a water tank in the trees. This is a zippy little option. By taking a right just before the water tank, you can ski down-

Directions at a glance

0.0 Leave trailhead, following signs for Hayes Copp Ski Trail.

0.7 Turn right on Great Gulf Link Trail.

1.3 Great Gulf Trail enters, bear right.

2.4 Turn right on Leavitt's Link Trail.

3.8 Hayes Copp Ski Trail reenters, stay straight and follow trail back to parking lot.

hill back to the campground road. Or ignore the option, go straight, and enjoy the ride back down to the parking lot.

How to get there

From Gorham travel south on Route 16 approximately 5 miles to the Pinkham "B" Road and turn left. Travel a few hundred yards and turn left to the plowed parking area at the Dolly Copp Campground.

From Glen travel north on Route 16 about 19 miles and turn left on the Pinkham "B" Road.

Mount Willard Trail

Crawford Notch, New Hampshire

Type of trail:	⬤⬤⬤⬤
Also used by:	Hikers
Distance:	1.6 miles one way; 3.2 miles round-trip
Terrain:	Flat, gradual incline
Trail difficulty:	Easiest
Surface quality:	Ungroomed
Food and facilities:	Snowshoe rentals, rest rooms, and water are available at the Appalachian Mountain Club's Crawford Notch Hostel, Route 302, Crawford Notch. Bring food and water on the trail. After the snowshoe tour try Fabyan's (603–278–2222) near Bretton Woods or the Red Parka Pub (603–383–4344) in Glen.
Phone numbers:	Crawford Notch Hostel (603–278–5170) or the Appalachian Mountain Club's Pinkham Notch Visitor Center (603–466–2721) for trail conditions; New Hampshire State Police, (800) 525–5555.

On a winter's day the views through Crawford Notch from the ledges of Mount Willard are unsurpassed. The eagle's eye panorama takes up the whole sky. In the distance Mount Chocorua's cone rises. A snake appears to be slithering along the valley floor, but that is no reptile. It's Route 302. The scars of a slide that killed the Willey family in 1826 is evident on the flanks of Mount Willey. In the east Mount Jackson stands firm; a glimpse of the Presidential Range and Mount Washington are your rewards for looking beyond Mount Jackson.

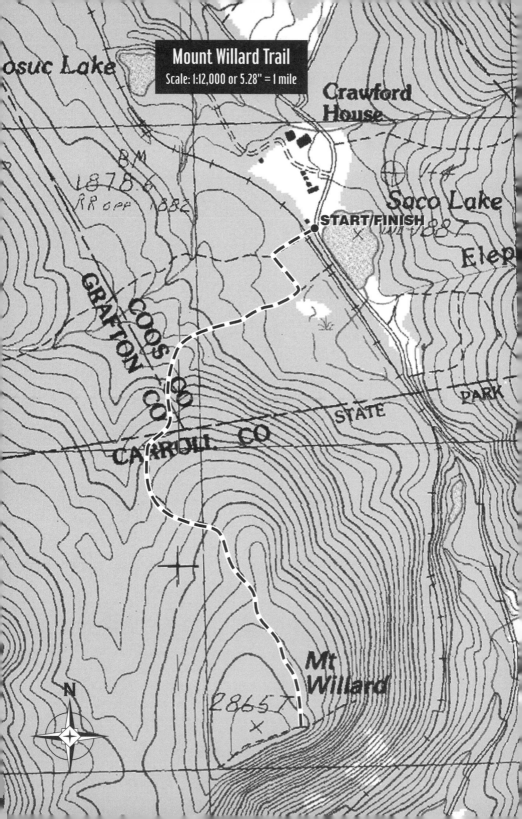

A sign points the way to the beginning of the Mount Willard Trail.

During summer and fall the Mount Willard Trail—maintained by the Appalachian Mountain Club—is a popular way up the 2,850-foot mountain. Your easy effort will yield rich and inspirational bounties. In winter the prize is equal. For those looking for a moonlight snowshoe trip, this is the one.

The trail by snowshoe is on the harder side of easy. The trailhead is across the road from Saco Lake, the source of the Saco River, which flows to the Atlantic. It is behind the brightly painted Crawford Depot, an information center during the nonsnow months. The old train station once served passengers going through the notch. In summer the Conway Scenic Railroad ends its run through the notch here. Past the tracks the trail begins with a flat walk in the woods.

The gradual ascent starts a short time later as the trail enters Crawford Notch State Park and follows a wide, carriage road, which at one time transported guests from the Crawford House, lost to a 1977 fire. At about the 0.5-mile mark, a sign points to the freezing waters of Centennial Pool off to the right. As the trail continues through the evergreens and birches, the wooded tops of two 4,000 footers—Mounts Tom and Field—can be spotted through the trees on the right. Near the top a trail to Hitchcock Flume enters from the left. From there it is just a few more yards to the vantage point. The views, on a clear day, burst out after you've snowshoed a trail sheltered by trees.

From the ledges look out through Crawford Notch, said to be discovered by a Lancaster hunter, Timothy Nash, during a 1771 moose hunt. The blemishes on Mount Willey are evident and are reminders of the tragic 1826 landslide. The Willey's, a family of seven with five children, lived by the base of Mount Willey. A drought that summer and the heavy rains that followed are thought to have triggered the rock slide. The family fled the house. The bodies of Samuel Willey, his wife, two children, and two boarders were found. Those of the three other children were not. Ironically the house withstood the storm. The Willey House site, a few miles from the Mount Willard trailhead, tells the history of the event.

Directions at a glance

0.0 Begin on the well-signed trail that leaves from behind the Crawford Notch Depot, some 125 yards from the Crawford Notch Hostel. The Mount Willard Trail follows the Avalon Trail for about 100 yards.

0.1 The trail bears left at a sign that reads MT. WILLARD. Some 100 yards later the trail bears right by a sign for Crawford Notch State Park

Follow the trail another 1.5 miles to the ledges.

1.6 Return along the same trail.

When out on the ledges, just be sure not to go too close to the edge. To return follow the same trail as it descends easily back to the trailhead.

How to get there

From I–93 take exit 35, Route 3, north to Twin Mountain; then Route 302 east to Crawford Notch. From Glen take Route 302 west to Crawford Notch. Park by the Crawford Notch Hostel.

Nineteen-Mile Brook Trail
Pinkham Notch, New Hampshire

Type of trail:	⬭
Also used by:	Hikers
Distance:	3.8 miles one way; 7.6 miles round-trip
Terrain:	Initally flat, then a gradual climb with a few steep pitches
Trail difficulty:	More difficult
Surface quality:	Ungroomed, but packed
Food and facilities:	Use the Appalachian Mountain Club's Carter Notch Hut, near the frozen shores of Carter Pond, to warm up, rest, and eat the food you have carried with you. Water is available, but carry extra. Hot water is also available, but carry tea, coffee, or hot chocolate. Overnight accommodations can be had, making this a welcome overnight experience (bring your own sleeping bag). The hut sleeps forty and has a caretaker in winter. Reservations are suggested.
Phone numbers:	Appalachian Mountain Club's Pinkham Notch Visitor Center (603–466–2721) for reservations for the hut; information from the U.S. Forest Service's Androscoggin Ranger Station, (603) 466–2713; New Hampshire State Police, (800) 525–5555.

To be in Carter Notch in winter is to experience a feeling of being remote and wild. The impressive pass between the 4,422-foot Wildcat Mountain and the 4,832-foot Carter Dome is the result of a glacial tug-of-war, with huge ice sheets carving out the gap while shaking massive boulders from the tops of the surrounding peaks. In the notch are two frozen ponds—Upper and Lower Carter Ponds—surrounded and dwarfed by the foreboding landscape.

The Appalachian Mountain Club's Carter Notch Hut is at 3,290 feet above sea level and is sandwiched between the two ponds. When the frigid winds blow, the hut is a welcome sanctuary. The AMC first built a small log cabin in the notch in 1904. It was replaced by a stone hut in 1914. It is said the present hut is haunted by the ghost of a former caretaker, "Red Mac" MacGregor.

Because of the hut this snowshoe trip (skiers can attempt this trail, but it is steep in places and the sporadic drainages may interrupt rhythm) is a natural for an overnight. The bunkhouse, adjacent to the hut, which is warmed by a woodstove, is unheated. Therefore if you are using backpacks, bring sleeping bags rated to at least minus 20 degrees.

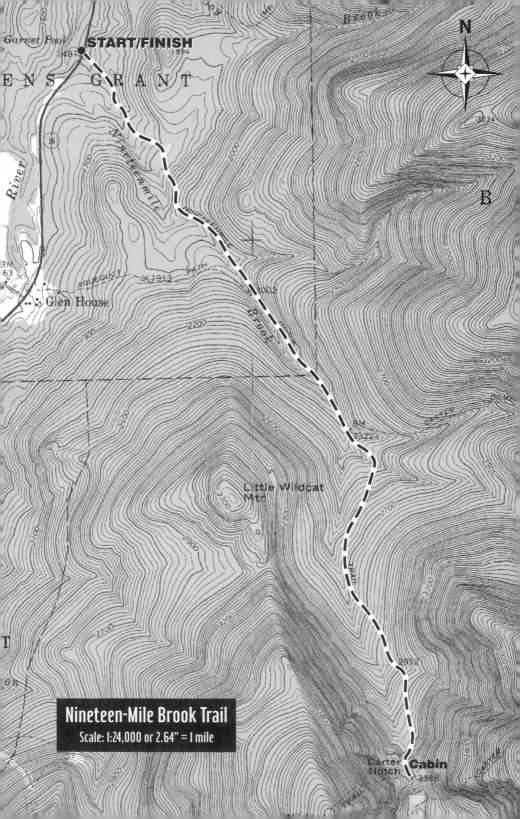

The Nineteen-Mile Brook Trail, which is well marked and leaves from the trailhead on Route 16, is also popular with winter hikers. Though the trail is ungroomed, it is the combination of hikers and snowshoers that packs it down. Midweek travelers will likely relish the solitude. Weekenders will likely have more company.

Not only is the trail popular, but the brook itself is also worth experiencing. It is a beautiful site as it rises easily through the forest. The brook's chilled waters form pools in certain spots, trapped by the boulders that stand in its path.

As the trail continues it narrows and come very close to the water's edge. Portions of the path near the brook can become icy during winter, so caution is suggested. A small hut and stone dam can be seen at about the 1.2-mile mark as the trail rises up above the waters. You cross several drainages before reaching the midway point. The Carter Dome Trail will diverge from the left at 1.9 miles, marking midway to Carter Notch.

Following the junction with the Carter Dome Trail, the trail begins to climb, steeply at times. You'll have to negotiate two narrow footbridges over the course of about 0.3 mile.

Through the trees spot the ridges of Wildcat Mountain. Steep pitches alternate with a few flat spots as the trail reaches its highest point at the 3.6-mile mark. Here Wildcat Ridge Trail enters.

Nineteen-Mile Brook Trail takes a sharp left and drops steeply through the firs. It is here that nature raises its curtain on a dramatic scene. From the woods the stage is set for a view of the western shores of Upper Carter Pond. Wildcat Mountain rises up like a giant wall. The trail hugs the bank and then reenters the woods where you'll pass the Carter-Moriah Trail. A few steps take you out to the northwest edge of Lower Carter Pond. Look up in the natural amphitheater and see the crags of Carter Dome. Just to the right of the dome is Pulpit Rock, still defying gravity.

Directions at a glance

0.0 Leave the trailhead via the Nineteen-Mile Brook Trail.

1.2 Spot a dam by the brook.

1.9 Carter Dome Trail enters from the left. Continue straight. Cross two narrow footbridges over the next 0.3 mile.

3.6 Turn left on the Nineteen-Mile Brook Trail, which drops steeply.

3.8 Carter-Moriah Trail enters from the left. Continue on the Nineteen-Mile Brook Trail.

3.9 Reach the hut. Stay the night or return via the same trail.

The Carter Notch Hut, though allegedly haunted, is a welcome stop on the Nineteen-Mile Brook Trail.

Snowshoers reach the hut after the second pond. Inside they can warm and refuel themselves before hunkering down for the night or returning along the same trail, which is right outside the hut's door.

How to get there

From Glen travel 16 miles north on Route 16. The trailhead is on the right. From Gorham travel about 7 miles south on Route 16. The trail-head is on the left.

Great Angel Loop/Great Glen Trails
Pinkham Notch, New Hampshire

Type of trail:	▬▬ ◄ ⬤
Distance:	4.2 miles
Terrain:	Flat to rolling
Trail difficulty:	More difficult
Surface quality:	Groomed, skate, double tracked
Food and facilities:	Rentals (ski and snowshoe), lessons, a wax room, restaurant, yurts, retail shop, and tubing are all found at Great Glen (with water and complimentary hot chocolate at the yurts). Restrooms are outside of the yurts. In addition Great Glen offers a Snowcat Shuttle service to the 4-mile mark on the Mount Washington Auto Road for a free-heel ski down the road. There is a fee to use the ski center trails. After skiing it's possible to dine at the timber base lodge or try the Red Parka Pub (603–383–4344) in Glen.
Phone numbers:	Great Glen Trails, (603) 466–2333.

They say location is everything. Great Glen Trails is located at the base of one of the most picturesque spots in New Hampshire—Mount Washington. The highest peak in the northeastern United States serves as a backdrop along with a few of its more dramatic sidekicks, Mounts Jefferson, Adams, and Monroe. Throw in wide, open meadows with winding, well-groomed runs through the beech, birch, and pines; views of the jagged Moriah-Carter Range to the east; vistas of the alpine slopes of Wildcat Mountain; and a couple of woodstove-heated yurts, and you've got the makings for winter fun.

Great Glen Trails opened on December 26, 1994. There are about 12 miles of skate and tracked trails. Snowshoes are allowed on all of the trails plus the 12 miles of backcountry trails that border the Great Gulf Wilderness on a side of Mount Washington. Only a small portion of the groomed network is classified as most difficult. The system is well signed. Trail names are given in both English and French. The trail names are a bit humorous and clever, too. There's the Great Grumpy Grade, which got its name because the trail took a bit longer to construct than anticipated, annoying the construction crew, which became a tad grumpy during work. Dragon Corridor got its name because with its twists, turns, and bumps, it resembles a dragon's tail.

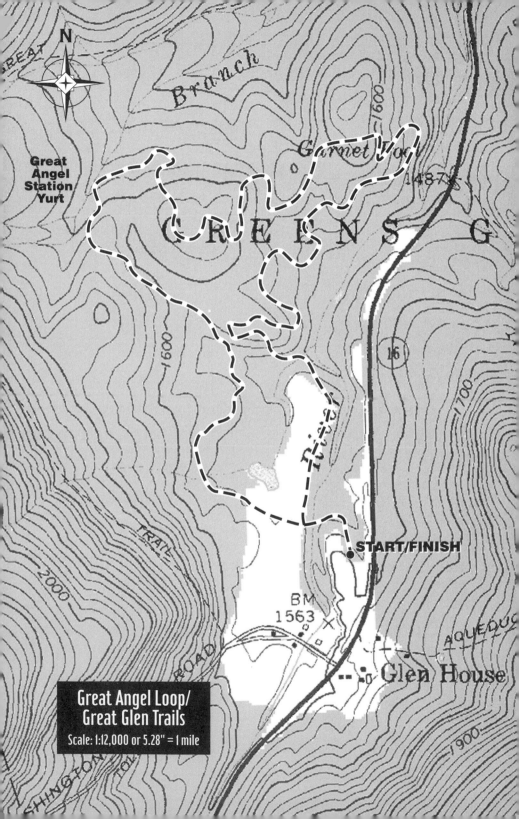

N

GREAT Branch

Garnet Pool

1487'

Great
Angel
Station
Yurt

G R E E N S G

1600

16

1600

1700

River

2000

TRAIL

START/FINISH

ROAD

BM
1563

AQUEDUC

Glen House

Great Angel Loop/
Great Glen Trails
Scale: 1:12,000 or 5.28" = 1 mile

1900

HINGTON TOL

With the Presidentials as a backdrop, the groomed trails of Great Glen Trails are pathways to adventure.

Great Angel Loop is named after the Great Angel Station yurt just off the Libby Trace and Dragon Corridor Trails. Located about one-third of the way into the flat to rolling circuit, the yurt offers warmth on cold days and a deck with picnic tables on those spring mornings. The loop is a collection of many easy and more difficult trails. The difficulty is not in the ascents—they are gradual—but in the exhilarating and winding downhills.

From the lodge the easy Geepers Trail leads to Great Meadows Sluice, which crosses over the flowing Peabody River and is the gateway to the ski system. Sluice links to Great Grumpy Grade, which offers stunning vistas of the snow-topped and craggy northern Presidentials from the flats of an alpine meadow. Grumpy enters the woods and hands off to Libby Trace by a huge granite slab called Coffee Pot Rock. Dawdle a bit at the rock and look at the old coffee pots on it. They were found when the trail system was built. By the way Libby Trace is named after Elihu Libby. He bought the Auto Road in 1906, and his descendants still own the road and Great Glen. Libby is a gradual rollick to Great Angel Station, where the deck serves up views of the neighboring wilderness area in the White Mountain National Forest.

The snakelike Dragon Corridor is next. Slay the trail by riding the winding path where bear, moose, and bobcat have been spotted. Dragon Corridor weaves into Peacemaker and Thumper. Both these trails drop and climb dramatically. Thumper has a picnic table for those who want to rest a bit after the roller coaster ride.

Wishbone Slip is like a switchback, the U-shaped turn provides excitment right into Hairball Passage. Hairball passes over a swampy area and gets its name from the population of snowshoe hares that frequents the area.

A short jaunt back on the Dragon Corridor leads to the flat and open Clementine Wash, which parallels the Peabody River, a drainage flowing out of Pinkham Notch and into the Androscoggin River. Clementine flows back to Sluice, which is the path back to the lodge.

Directions at a glance

0.0 Leave the lodge on Geepers Trail.

0.2 Turn left at Glen Meadows Sluice.

0.4 Continue on Great Grumpy Grade.

0.7 Turn right on Libby Trace.

1.4 Bear right on Dragon Corridor. Great Angel Station is by the intersection.

1.9 Bear left on Peacemaker.

2.1 Bear right on Thumper.

2.9 Continue straight on Wishbone Slip.

3.2 Turn left on Hairball Passage.

3.3 Turn left on Dragon Corridor.

3.4 Turn right on Clementine Wash.

3.8 Turn left on Glen Meadows Sluice.

4.0 Turn right on Geepers and travel 0.2 mile to lodge.

How to get there

From North Conway, New Hampshire, travel west on Routes 16/302 to Glen. Turn right at traffic light on Route 16 north and travel approximately 12 miles to Great Glen on the left. From Gorham, New Hampshire, travel south on Route 16 to Great Glen approximately 6 miles on the right.

Fire Tower Trail

Phillips Brook Backcountry Recreation Area, Odell, New Hampshire

Type of trail:	⬭ ▬
Also used by:	Hikers, backcountry skiers, dogsledders
Distance:	5.6 miles round-trip
Terrain:	Flat to hilly
Trail difficulty:	More difficult
Surface quality:	Groomed after snowstorms
Food and facilities:	There are portable toilets at the field office for day users. No water is available on the trail. There are toilets at the five yurts in the area. Stop in Gorham or Berlin at the many grocery stores for food. A fire tower makes an ideal spot for a knapsack lunch. After the outing consider the lunch and dinner buffets at the Golden Maple (603–466–2766) on Main Street in Gorham.
Phone numbers:	Phillips Brook Backcountry Recreation Area, (800) 872–4578.

Near the roof of New Hampshire is a place where the moose, deer, and fisher mingle with the logger, snowshoer, backcountry skier, and sled dog driver. It is called the Phillips Brook Backcountry Recreation Area and is a unique partnership on 24,000 acres in the remote northern section of the state called the Great North Woods.

In 1997 a North Conway, New Hampshire, company called Mountain Recreation entered into an agreement with International Paper for rights to operate the recreation area on land owned by the paper company. While loggers continue their harvest, backcountry enthusiasts can play on the land that abuts the state's 45,000-acre Nash Stream State Forest.

Skiers and snowshoers are given free access to the trails, which are primarily logging roads and multiuse trails. Mountain Recreation makes its money by running a lodge and network of yurts that

Makeshift signs point the way at the Phillips Brook Backcountry Recreation Area.

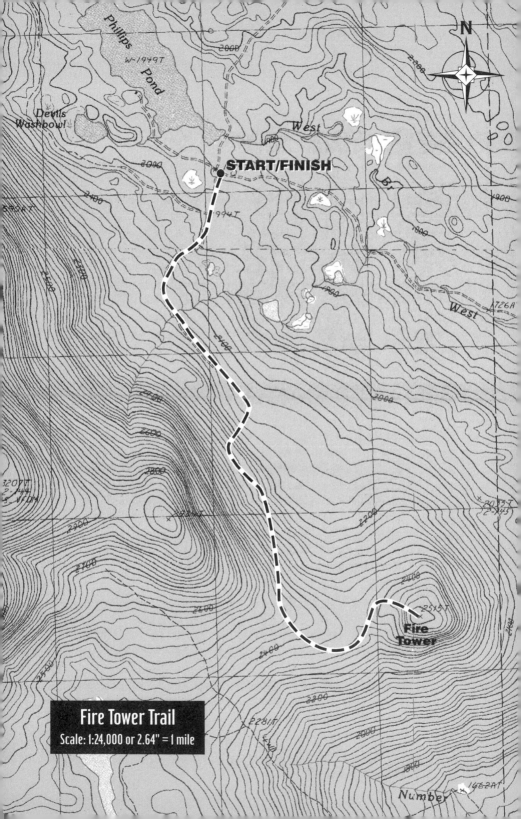

N

Phillips Pond

W-1949T

Devils
Washbowl

West

START/FINISH

994T

West

Br

West

1726A

**Fire
Tower**

2515T

2408

Fire Tower Trail
Scale: 1:24,000 or 2.64" = 1 mile

Number

1662AT

skiers, hikers, and showshoers can use. During the nonsnow months, mountain bikers and hikers use the miles of trails and yurts.

Make no mistake, this is a remote, backcountry experience. Even getting to the trailheads can be an adventure for some along a snow-covered dirt road. Logging gates are sometimes locked, and the combinations must be obtained from the Phillips Brook field office before recreationalists can proceed.

The trails are well defined through grooming and use; however, do not use the multicolored plastic ribbons tied to the trees as trail markers. These flags are used by the paper company to indicate harvest areas and proposed routes.

Directions at a glance

0.0 Leave the trailhead on the Trio Ponds Trail.

2.1 Turn right on the Trio Ponds Trail at the junction with the Gorge Trail.

2.4 Turn left on the Fire Tower Trail and travel 0.4 mile to the fire tower.

2.8 Return via the same route.

While out on the trails, keep an eye out for wildlife. Even if you do not spot some creatures, it is commonplace to spot the deep tracks of a moose or their round droppings.

The outing begins with a gradual ascent throught the hardwood forest on the northeast side of Whitcomb Mountain. As elevation increases, so does the damage done by the ice storm of January 1998. The storm's wrath was vengeful, splintering trees like toothpicks and toppling the crowns of many a hardwood. Birch trees seem to bow out of respect.

A traverse, with views across to Owl Head and Kelsey Mountains, takes skiers and snowshoers just below the saddle that connects the fire tower to the mountain. A few switchbacks later, you leave the Trio Ponds Trail for the winding Fire Tower Trail. (The Trio Ponds Trail is a fine choice for a side trip as it is 1.3 miles to Trio Ponds Yurt and an overnight backcountry experience).

The fire tower was built in the early 1950s by International Paper as a way to look out over the Phillips Brook Valley and keep an eye on company holdings. The wintry panaorama extends into the Mahoosucs of Maine and the Moriahs and regal Presidentials of New Hampshire to the south. Dummer and Trio Ponds glimmer in the distance.

The real fun for skiers begins on the return trip to the trailhead. The Fire Tower Trail twists and winds down moderately to the junction with the Trio Ponds Trail. The switchbacks are now a series of exhilarating S-turns. As the trip ends, the final third of a mile back to the trailhead is a wide cruise back to the road.

How to get there

From Berlin travel north approximately 18 miles to Paris Road in West Milan. Turn right on Paris Road and drive 3.5 miles to the Paris Road office of Timberland Trails. Four-wheel drive vehicles are recommended during winter travel. At the field office get the handout that provides the combinations to the gates along the road. Follow the signs to the Phillips Brook Lodge. The trailhead for the Trio Ponds Trail is approximately 10 miles in on the left.

Boulder Loop Trail
Albany, New Hampshire

Type of trail:	⬤⬤⬤⬤
Also used by:	Hikers
Distance:	3.0 miles
Terrain:	Hilly
Trail difficulty:	Easiest
Surface quality:	Ungroomed
Food and facilities:	Toilets are available at the winter parking area. No water is available during the loop. You can rent snowshoes at the Kancamagus Snowshoe Center (Baldy's) on Route 112, Conway, (603) 447–5287. You can do your grocery shopping in Conway. After the loop try the Alpenglow Grill, Main Street, Conway, (603) 447–5524. You'll need a White Mountain National Forest Recreation Pass to park in the winter parking area.
Phone numbers:	White Mountain National Forest's Saco Ranger District, (603) 447–5448.

The Boulder Loop Trail is a shining example of how a popular summer and fall hike can turn into an excellent winter snowshoe excursion. The 3.0-mile trail rewards the snowshoer with spectacular vistas above the Passaconaway Valley for a relatively modest amount of effort. Not only that, the mammoth glaciers that moved through the area some 50,000 years ago left large, granite boulders behind that are transformed into towering jewels of ice in winter. One of the massive slabs measures 30 feet high and 100 feet long. There is even one spot on the loop where it is possible to snowshoe under a boulder for a cavelike experience.

The yellow-blazed trail reaches its highest point after about a 1,000-foot climb through the spruce, fir, oak, and maple. On the downside of

N

START/FINISH

Camp ground

SWIFT

Covered Bridge

R

112

1300

1200

1100

894

898

860

1300

the loop, ash and hemlock trees make up portions of the landscape. Numbered posts are scattered through the trail. They correspond with a pamphlet put out by the U.S. Forest Service that describes the history of the glacial activity and ecology of the area. Lichens, a combination of fungus and algae, grow on the boulders. The plants emit an acid that seeps through the rock, breaking it down, one of the first steps in producing soil. Nature's wrath in the form of a nor'easter is evident in some of the uprooted trees. Stumps are all that remain from timber sales of the 1940s. Tree crowns have been snapped by the ice storm of 1998.

The trail leaves Passaconaway Road and comes to a junction after just 0.2 mile. Taking the loop in the clockwise direction brings snowshoers alongside the boulders on a moderate climb. The trail takes a hard right by a large smooth rock face and follows it for a short spell. The trail will then take a hard left into a mixed hardwood and evergreen forest and by some blowdowns.

Wonderful views are yours to experience as the trail advances to an overlook. Look to the south where the weaving Kancamagus Highway and winding Swift River run below. The rocky cone of Mount Chororua is in the distance.

The trail takes a hard left and reenters the woods. At about 1.5 miles a spur trail leads to the ledges. Use good judgment here. It's a short scamper to the ledges with views of the Passaconaway Valley and Mounts Passaconaway and Chororua. Do not get close to the edge of the cliffs. The views are just as fine from a safe vantage point.

Directions at a glance

0.0   Leave the trailhead for the Boulder Loop Trail.

0.2   Turn left at the sign saying LEDGES 1.3 MILES.

1.5   Option exists to turn right for a 0.1-mile snowshoe to a scenic overlook. Or continue 1.3 miles on Boulder Loop Trail.

2.8   Continue straight at junction with LEDGES sign and return to trailhead.

The main trail curves around the ledges and begins its descent. It's not all downhill at this point, so be prepared for a dip or two before heading back down to the boulders and crossing a small brook. The trail returns to the junction and then back to the road.

How to get there

From Conway travel south on Route 16 about a half mile. Turn right (west) on Route 112, the Kancamagus Highway. Travel 2.5 miles and turn right on Passaconaway Road. Park in the winter parking area to the right. To reach the trailhead walk over the covered bridge and bear right. The trailhead is on the left, a short way down.

Echo Lake Trail

Echo Lake State Park, North Conway, New Hampshire

Type of trail:	
Also used by:	Walkers, hikers, snowmobilers
Distance:	1.0-mile loop
Terrain:	Flat
Trail difficulty:	Easiest
Surface quality:	Ungroomed, but packed
Food and facilities:	The facilities at Echo Lake State Park—like water and restrooms—are dormant during winter. Bring all supplies you'll need. Nearby North Conway village is a spot to rent cross-country skis or snowshoes. After the trip Hooligan's (603–356–6110) on Kearsarge Street is a good dining choice.
Phone numbers:	New Hampshire Division of Parks and Recreation, (603) 271–3556; Carroll County Sheriff's Department, for emergencies only, (800) 552–8960.

The flat Lake Trail in Echo Lake State Park is a pleasant and easy trek along the edge of a frozen lake. The 1.0-mile loop never strays far from water's view and offers both views of distant Mount Kearsarge North and the striking climbing ledges—White Horse and Cathedral. The two ledges, where rock climbers scale granite in summer and fall, and ice climbers play their slippery game in winter, dwarf the small lake.

Popular in summer as a hiking and mountain biking trail, the Lake Trail maintains a certain degree of charm during the snow months. It isn't unusual to come across walkers and their dogs, or even a slow-moving snowmobile, during an outing on the pine-laden trail. Though this trail is used by snowmobiles, snowshoers and skiers can get around this by just circumnavigating the lake when the ice is sufficiently thick and solid.

The snow covers the emerald green waters of the lake and its sandy shores. Reminders of summer are everywhere as snowshoers and skiers move past the dormant bathhouses and the snow-covered picnic tables, some propped on their sides. It is the lifeguard chair, bright orange, that

Directions at a glance

0.0 From the gate by the park, enter in the unplowed parking area and head for the gatehouse. At about 200 feet turn right at the gatehouse.

0.1 Turn right on the Lake Trail and follow it around the lake. The trail returns to the unplowed parking lot.

is a draw. Climb in and be king of winter's domain in the forest of oak and pine. Straight ahead are the magnificent cliffs called White Horse Ledge. It might take some imagination, but try to spot the horse. To the left are the tips of the Moat Range. You can see the upper section of a hotel built under the ledge, too. Over to the right is the rounded top of Cathedral Ledge. Binoculars are a good idea to try and spot the ice climbers.

Winter hikers often carry snowshoes.

It may be enough for some visitors to just ski or snowshoe across the ice. But the trail is easy and flat. Because of its ease, the excursion is a prime candidate for families with children or newcomers to Nordic skiing and snowshoeing. This trail is particularly enjoyable after a fresh snow. It can harden up some after a famed New England thaw though.

Though the trail can be done in either direction, we go counterclockwise from the beach. Soon, an unsigned trail forks to the right; stay to the left on the Lake Trail, which hugs the shore. The trail rounds the lake and soon a sign points to the Bryce Path on the right. Stay nearest to the shore. Keep on eye on the lifeguard chair. When you are directly across from it, look up to the left and see Mount Kearsarge North. On its top stands a fire tower.

The trail heads away from the shores for a tad and comes to another sign that indicates you are on the Echo Lake Trail. Just after that, a path emerges from the left and leads to the shores of the lake. Stay straight to go to the unplowed parking area and return to your car.

How to get there

From North Conway travel on River Road for approximately 1 mile. Turn right on West Side Road. Turn right a half mile later on Echo Lake Road, following the signs to the park entrance.

Lincoln Woods/Pemi East Side Road Trails

Lincoln, New Hampshire

Type of trail:	
Also used by:	Hikers
Distance:	11.0-mile loop
Terrain:	Flat
Trail difficulty:	Easiest, more difficult
Surface quality:	Packed, double tracked
Food and facilities:	Information center, rest rooms, water, and hot chocolate are available at the trailhead. Several shops in Lincoln rent skis and snowshoes. The nearest food is available in Lincoln, where you'll find The Common Man (603–745–3463), an enjoyable spot for a meal.
Phone numbers:	Pemigewasset Ranger Station in Plymouth, (603) 536–1310 (It is advised to check in with a ranger at the information center at the trailhead before heading into the Pemigewasset wilderness area or to find out about frozen river crossings.); New Hampshire State Police, (800) 525–5555.

The Lincoln Woods Cross-Country Ski Trails are a mellow winter playground for cross-country skiers and snowshoers. This is one of the most popular winter trail destinations in the White Mountain National Forest. The U.S. Forest Service maintains about 8 miles of trails here, tracking and packing them after a sizeable snowfall. The trails are on opposite sides of the East Branch of the Pemigewasset River, yet both are double tracked with a lane in the middle. Skiers take the tracks. Snowshoers and hikers take the middle. The Lincoln Woods Trail, on the west side, is an ideal spot for families and first-timers. At its beginning it crosses a 160-foot suspension bridge. The trail then follows a straight line along an old railroad grade to a stone wall at a bridge over Franconia Brook. Along the way the Pemigewasset, with its browns, whites, green, and brackish colors of winter, offers a soothing vista. The stone wall is a delightful place to stop for lunch. Be prepared for aerial visits from the birds that frequent the area. From here it is a short half-mile jaunt along the Franconia Falls Trail, which parallels the brook to Franconia Falls along an old logging road. Or, take the Black Pond Trail, which first skirts Ice Pond, where block ice was cut during logging days, and then advances to the panorama of Black Pond. Both trails are rated more difficult and are narrow.

START/FINISH

Lincoln Woods/Pemi
East Side Road Trails
Scale: 1:48,000 or 1.32" = 1 mile

The Pemi East Side Road Trail, deemed more difficut, runs along the east side of the river on a forest road with a few hills. It ends at a gate that is the boundary for the wilderness area. About 1.0 mile into the trail, look for views of Mount Bond in the distance and then at about the 2.5-mile mark a panorama of Franconia Ridge. A fun option is to take the easy Pine Island Trail, which is about a half mile into East Side. The narrow 0.8-mile trail through red pine bypasses the first hill before rejoining the East Side. There is a spot by the gated boundary to the wilderness area where skiers and shoers are tempted to cross the ice and continue a loop on the Lincoln Woods Trail. This crossing is not recommended.

However there is a way to combine both the Lincoln Woods and East Side Trails for an 11.0-mile backcountry loop suitable for better skiers and snowshoers. Follow the East Side Trail until you reach the gated boundary of the wilderness area and continue past the gate. The trail is now called the Wilderness Trail, and it is not maintained by the Forest Service. Instead the tracks are made by skiers passing through. There are several vantage points from which to view the river, but then the trail heads east and away

Directions at a glance

0.0 Follow the Pemi East Side Road Trail.

2.9 Continue straight past gate to wilderness area.

5.0 Bear left at signed junction with Cedar Brook Trail.

5.5 Cross suspension bridge and make left on Wilderness Trail, which becomes Lincoln Woods Trail.

11.0 Turn left at suspension bridge. First left, then the first right leads back to information center and parking area.

from the rushing waters. It is on this stretch that several small water run-offs must be crossed. The amount of snow will determine the width of the crossings. The trail crosses Cedar Brook and soon climbs steeply to a junction with the signed Cedar Brook Trail. From there it is about a half mile to a suspension bridge that spans the river. The west side of the river is much flatter and is a virtual straight shot all the way along a railroad grade. In less than 1.0 mile, you pass an old trestle across a bridge. There is a slight dip before the bridge. The trail then passes a junction with the Bondcliff Trail. When reaching the bridge over Franconia Brook, there is only about 2.8 miles left. An option exists here for side excursions to the falls and Black Pond. The trail will leave the river's edge, heading away from it. Pass a campsite, its status in flux due to overuse. The trail returns with river views after it passes the Osseo Trail. Finally the loop ends after crossing the suspension bridge that leads back to the trailhead.

How to get there

The Lincoln Woods Cross-Country Ski Trails are located about 5 miles east of I–93, exit 32, on the Kancamagus Highway (Route 112).

Around-Lonesome-Lake Trail
Franconia, New Hampshire

Type of trail:	(icon)
Also used by:	Hikers
Distance:	3.2 miles
Terrain:	Hilly, flat
Trail difficulty:	More difficult
Surface quality:	Ungroomed
Food and facilities:	No facilities, except for a pay phone, exist at the trailhead. Winter camping without facilities is available at the Lafayette Place Campground (603–271–3556). Close by is the Cannon Mountain ski area, at exit 2 off Franconia Notch Parkway (603–823–5563). Snowshoe rentals (603–823–5563) are available at Cannon Mountain, as are rest rooms and a cafeteria. Also of note: You can take a round-trip tram ride to the top of the 4,100-foot peak to snowshoe the 0.5-mile Rim Trail. Tickets are available at the base lodge. The New England Ski Museum (603–823–7177) is next to the base area and well worth a visit. After the trip consider Chieng Gardens (603–745–8612) on Main Street in Lincoln.
Phone numbers:	Franconia Notch State Park, (603) 823–5563; New Hampshire State Police, (800) 525–5555.

One of the finest snowshoe trips in the White Mountains is a trek to the serene shores of Lonesome Lake in Franconia Notch State Park. The lake sits in a basin under the twin peaks of 4,293-foot North Kinsman and the 4,358-foot South Kinsman. But the prize in this jaunt is the dazzling beauty of the Franconia Ridge. The snow-choked ravines are like fingers between the crusty ridges. During a day of sunshine, the combination of the wind-drifted snow on the frozen lake, the Kinsman pair, and the Franconias are like a perfectly executed oil painting. One must reach out and touch to see if it is real.

The snowshoe trek begins at the well-signed Lonesome Lake Trailhead. The trailhead is also used by snowmobilers riding the paved bike

Around-Lonesome-Lake Trail
Scale: 1:12,000 or 5.28" = 1 mile

A skier enjoys the solitude.

path through the notch. Begin by taking a hand-railed footbridge over the Pemigewasset, crossing the Pemi Trail, and passing through the sleeping campground along the yellow-blazed trail.

After leaving the campground the trail begins a long, moderate climb of 1,000 feet through the hardwoods over a series of switchbacks. Cross a small wooden bridge over a brook at about 0.3 mile and then one more bridge shortly thereafter. At about 0.4 mile the Hi-Cannon Trail enters right. For the most part the trail follows an old bridle path. As it winds its way up the ridge, it is sometimes narrow. While resting, look behind through the birch to see the sparkling Franconia Range.

The forest changes as the ascent continues. Soon evergreens reign. The sounds of the traffic rolling along the road below are a memory. Quiet takes over during a short dip to a junction near the edge of the lake. It is here that the Cascade Trail heads left and the Dodge Cut-off goes right. A small path at the junction heads down to the eastern shore of the lake.

Now you must make a decision. If it is sunny and the lake is sufficiently frozen, it is a pleasure to snowshoe directly across the lake to the Appalachian Mountain Club's Lonesome Lake Hut on the southwest shores. Look closely and you will see the cabins from the eastern shore.

However there is an option of taking the Around-Lonesome-Lake Trail, an 0.8-mile loop. The trail is flat and is made up of a number of different trails. The downside of this trail is that portions of it pass through boggy sections that are traversed by narrow log bridges.

Take the Around-Lonesome-Lake Trail by making a left on the Lonesome Lake Trail. The blue-blazed trail nears the shore, and after 0.2 mile, the Around-Lonesome-Lake Trail bears right. After that the Fishin' Jimmy Trail (part of the Appalachian Trail) enters. Take it and bear right, cross a log bridge over a stream, and start to look for the snow-covered sandy beach.

Across the water is an awe-inspiring view—the Franconias. From left to right there are Mount Lafayette at 5,260 feet, Mount Lincoln at 5,089 feet, and Little Haystack Mountain at 4,760 feet.

At the beach there is a sign pointing to the Lonesome Lake Hut. The hut, at about 2,760 feet, was built in 1964 and is open from May to October.

These shores are an ideal lunch spot. The Fishin' Jimmy Trail continues to round the lake. It crosses the brooks and bogs of the western shore at fine vantage points. It also crosses numerous narrow bridges.

Bear right on the Cascade Brook Trail as the path reenters the woods and then meets the junction of the Lonesome Lake Trail again. You have been here before. Take one last look at the lake before heading left on the Lonesome Lake Trail.

Directions at a glance

0.0 Leave via Lonesome Lake Trail.

0.4 Hi-Cannon Trail enters from the right.

1.2 There is a four-way junction at the pond's edge. Turn left for Around-Lonesome-Lake Trail via Cascade Brook Trail.

1.4 Bear left on Around-Lonesome-Lake Trail.

1.6 Continue straight on Fishin' Jimmy Trail.

1.8 Bear right on Cascade Brook Trail.

2.0 Turn left on Lonesome Lake Trail and descend the 1.2-mile trail to the parking area.

The descent doesn't appear to be as long as the ascent. Try to snatch a glimpse of the Franconias on the way down if you can stop looking at your feet. The familiar trail snakes downward, through the campground and back to the parking area.

How to get there

From the south exit the Franconia Notch State Parkway at the sign for Lafayette Place Campground. Turn left in the parking area. An underpass will lead to the other side of the road and the trailhead.

From the north exit the Franconia Notch State Parkway at the sign for Lafayette Place Campground. The trailhead is opposite the brown visitor center.

Lower Nanamocomuck Ski Trail
Albany, New Hampshire

Type of trail:	▬▬▬ ⬭
Also used by:	Hikers
Distance:	6.9 miles one way
Terrain:	Flat, rolling
Trail difficulty:	Easiest to more difficult
Surface quality:	Ungroomed, skier tracked
Food and facilities:	Toilets are available at trail's end in the Albany Covered Bridge parking area, but food and water are not. This trail system is not patrolled by the U.S. Forest Service. After the ski stop in Conway at Cafe Noche (603–447–5050).
Phone numbers:	For the latest trail conditions, the Saco Ranger station, (603) 447–5448; for emergencies, the Carroll County Sheriff's Department, (800) 552–8960.

The Lower Nanamocomuck Ski Trail parallels the boulder-strewn Swift River, affording skiers and snowshoers miles of opportunities for adventure. This is a gem of a trail because there are an incredible number of vistas and trail options. The Swift River itself is stunning. The trail runs along its length for a good portion of the route, cuts back into the forest, then comes back to water's edge. At Rocky Gorge skiers and shoers can choose to visit the quiet, frozen shores of Falls Pond and gaze up among the spruce and pine to see Bear Mountain, or they can cross a bridge to see the roiling waters of the gorge against walls of granite. (Remove your skis before entering the Rocky Gorge area because there are steps and the bridge crossing for those who go to view the rushing waters.) There is one more option here. The Lovequist Loop, a 0.7-mile trail around Falls Pond, is an ideal spot for snowshoeing in either direction because it swings between forest and shore.

Along the trail there are a few loop options to consider as well. The Wenonah and Wenunchus Ski Trails—spurs off the Lower Nanamocomuck—can be skied in either direction. Here are grueling climbs and exhilarating downhills for the more advanced skier. These two trails later rejoin the Lower Nanamocomuck.

Now a few words about all those Native American names. Many of the peaks in the White Mountains are named after the Indians who once lived in the area. Kancamagus, "The Fearless One," was chief of the Penacook tribe in the 1680s. His father was Nanamocomuck. Wenonah happened to be the daughter of Chocorua and the wife of Wonalancet, while

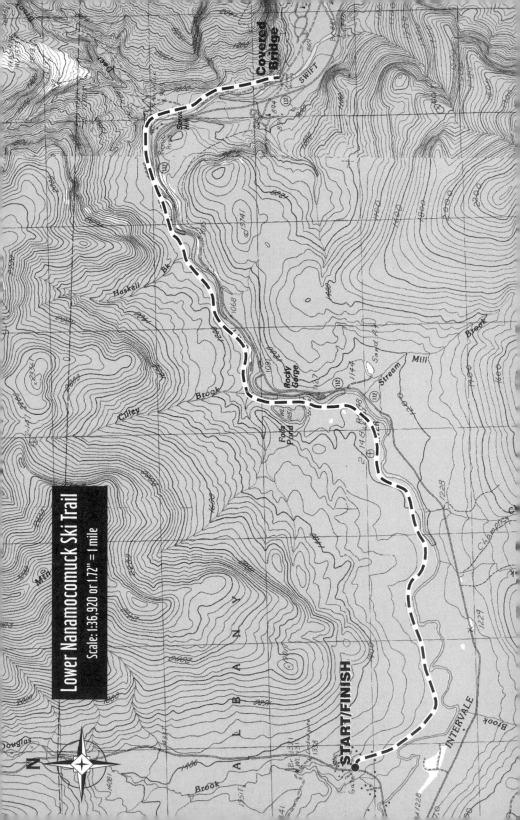

Wenunchus was the daughter of Passaconway and sister of Nanamoco-muck. Don't worry, there isn't a quiz.

Though the Lower Nanamocomuck is rated easiest, it should not be attempted by beginner skiers who are out for a first outing. There are sections where snow-plow and herringbone or sidestepping skills are necessary. As for snowshoers, please try and stay off the ski tracks.

Throughout the journey the trail is marked with blue, plastic dia-monds. There are nearly a dozen bridge crossings. Just try not to catch a pole in the gaps between the planks. Many signs tick off the miles, alert-ing trail-users to where they are. This journey is from east to west, drop-ping in elevation from 1,340 feet on Bear Notch Road to 880 feet by the covered bridge.

The initial section of the trail is a bit bumpy and narrow through the evergreens. Depending on the amount of snowfall, there are some wet areas that you'll tra-verse. But shortly thereafter you'll enounter the first of many down-hill bursts. The trail eventually makes its way to the banks of the Swift River, where it rolls along its edges. The snow attempts to cover examples of the erosion that has taken place over the years. After about 2.5 miles—past sev-eral spots at which to gaze and ponder—the trail takes a hard left and begins a twisting climb up through the forest before submit-ting to gravity. The trail descends to a junction with the Wenonah Trail. Now head to Rocky Gorge, more than midway on this jaunt. It is here that skiers climb rather steeply only to have to ride down again. These hills might prove too much for some beginner skiers. Take off your skis, particularly if condi-tions are icy, and walk to where you can spot Falls Pond and Rocky Gorge. Down the steps is the churning water. To the left is the peaceful shore. The loop around the pond is closed to cross-country skiers, but snowshoers can circumnavigate the shores.

Directions at a glance

0.0 Leave the parking area on the Lower Nanamocomuck Trail. There is a sign.

0.7 Turn right on the Lower Nanamocomuck. The Paugus Trail enters from the left.

3.5 Bear right on the Lower Nanamocomuck at the junction of the Wenonah Trail.

4.3 Bear right on the Lower Nanamocomuck toward the Covered Bridge campground. The Wenunchus Trail enters from the left.

6.0 Turn right on the Lower Nanamocomuck.

6.2 Turn right on Deer Brook Road (Forest Road 28), part of the Lower Nanamocomuck.

6.9 Turn right, go across the bridge to the parking area.

The Albany Covered Bridge is the ending point for a pleasant ski along the Lower Nanamoco-muck Ski Trail.

The Lower Nanamocomuck continues with a few more dips. The first descent after Rocky Gorge has a bridge near its bottom. It is easy to cross. Just be forewarned. The trail flattens out some and finds the Swift again as the Wenunchus Trail enters as an option.

Tiny drainages present some narrow crossings along the river bank, depending on the amount of snow. Use good judgment.

Once again the trail leaves water's edge to climb a bit into the forest. But it is now less than 2.0 miles to the covered bridge. Look down on the waters of the Swift after climbing a ridge. The route heads gently down to a junction where a wide forest road awaits. On Deer Brook Road a portion of the Lower Nanamocomuck, skiers are treated to something special. The last 1.0 mile of this tour is wide and an easy sloping downhill. Stop to admire the waters and vistas. When you spot the Albany covered bridge (1858), you are near trail's end. Head across the brown bridge to the parking area.

How to get there

To reach the Lower Nanamocomuck Ski Trailhead on Bear Notch Road in Bartlett, New Hampshire, travel on the Kancamagus Highway (Route 112) approximately 12 miles west of Conway and turn right on Bear Notch Road. Travel 1 mile and park in the plowed area. For the Albany Covered Bridge parking area, travel 6 miles west on the Kancamagus Highway from Conway and turn right on Passaconway Road.

The middle of the trail can be accessed via Rocky Gorge, which is about 8.5 miles west of Conway on the Kancamagus Highway. Parking is available at the east end of the Rocky Gorge Service Road. Snowshoers looking to walk the Lovequist Loop will begin here.

We suggest parking one car on Bear Notch Road and another at the covered bridge for this tour.

Old Bridle Path
Holderness, New Hampshire

Type of trail:	(icon)
Also used by:	Hikers
Distance:	0.9 mile one way; 1.8 miles round-trip
Terrain:	Hilly
Trail difficulty:	Easiest
Surface quality:	Ungroomed
Food and facilities:	There are no facilities. Both Meredith and Holderness have stores for last minute items. Try Guiseppe's (603–279–3313) at the Mill Falls Marketplace in Meredith for a pizza.
Phone numbers:	Squam Lakes Association, (603) 968–7336; Holderness Police for emergencies, (603) 968–3333.

The trip up West Rattlesnake by way of the Old Bridle Path is one of the best snowshoes in New Hampshire's Lakes Region. At 0.9 mile one way, this short and easy journey will reward you with its beautiful views. Beginners and families will no doubt be attracted to the path because of its ease. Those who look for more challenging terrain should not overlook this jaunt and shortchange themselves. On a day when you just want to get out for a couple of hours, or have slept in a bit, this is the one to choose.

The trail, an old carriage road, is blazed in yellow and is maintained by the Squam Lakes Association. The association says the trail is the most heavily used in the area. Once up at the 1,260-foot summit, the views south and west of Big Squam Lake and the surrounding mountains are nothing short of spectacular.

West Rattlesnake and neighboring East Rattlesnake are two small mountains on the northern edge of Squam Lake. While ascending the Old Bridle Path, and certainly during the descent, the silhouette of the Squam Range with Mounts Morgan and Percival is unmistakable.

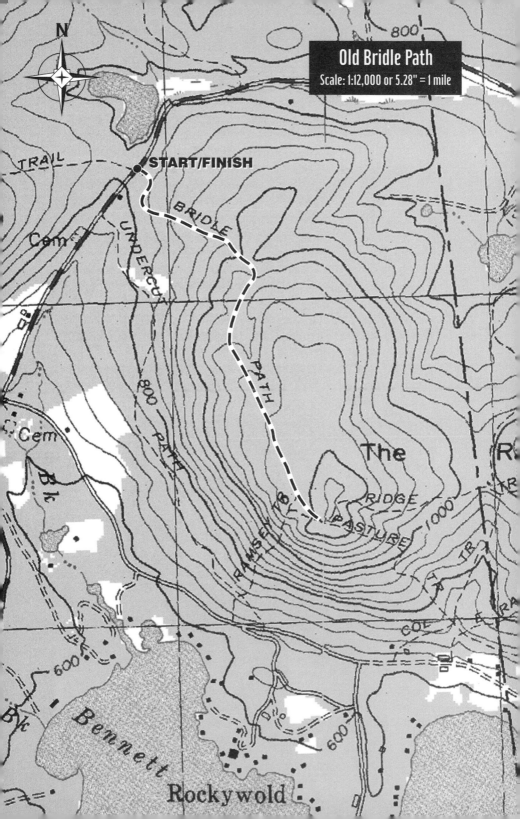

From the top and the open ledges, look down some 500 feet on the lake's many coves and islands. The state's largest lake, Winnipesaukee, is out in the distance. The peak with the fire tower is 2,384-foot Mount Belknap in Gilford. The flat slabs of rock at the summit are ideal spots for a lunch and a wonderful place to gather inspiration.

Squam Lake may bring back memories for snowshoers of a certain age. It was on those waters that the movie *On Golden Pond,* featuring Katharine Hepburn, Henry Fonda, and Jane Fonda, was filmed, bringing notoriety to the area.

Directions at a glance

0.0 Leave the trailhead for the Old Bridle Path to West Rattlesnake and travel 0.9 mile.

0.9 Reach summit.

Return the same way via Old Bridle Path to trailhead.

The Old Bridle Path is very easy to follow. From the parking lot cross Route 113 and turn right. It's a couple of hundred feet to the signed trailhead. The wide path is a gradual climb, with several flat spots for those who need a breather. Children will enjoy looking for trees that have been used as a construction zone by the pileated woodpecker.

There are those who might wish they had brought their skis for a trip downhill from the summit. The Squam Lakes Association does not recommend this trail for skiing.

How to get there

From Meredith travel on Routes 3 north/25 west from the traffic lights at the junction with Route 16. Drive 8.0 miles and turn right on Route 113 in Holderness heading east. At 5.6 miles turn left into the trail parking area. The trail is across the street and to the right.

Ellis River Trail

Jackson, New Hampshire

Type of trail:	▬▬ ◄
Distance:	15.5 miles
Terrain:	Flat to hilly
Trail difficulty:	Easiest to most difficult
Surface quality:	Single tracked, double tracked, skate
Food and facilities:	Instruction, rentals, rest rooms, trail passes, wax room, and advice are available from the Jackson Ski Touring Foundation headquarters and the adjacent Jack Frost Ski Shop. A warming hut is located on the Ellis River Trail. For skiing the Ellis River Trail one way, shuttle service is available on weekends from its terminus at the Dana Place Inn. Spotting a second car at the inn will suffice during midweek. There are a number of inns and restaurants in Jackson, including the Red Fox Pub (603–383–6659) and Jackson Bistro (603–383–6633), for after-ski meals.
Phone numbers:	Jackson Ski Touring Foundation, (603) 383–9355 or (800) XC–SNOWS.

Sometimes it's just hard to choose which trail to ski at a cross-country ski center. That can happen in Jackson, New Hampshire. When it does, try this long loop, which features three of the system's trails—Ellis River, High Water, and the Hall.

The Ellis River Trail is a favorite among White Mountain trails. The trail runs through evergreens and hardwoods close to the waters of the west bank of the Ellis River, its 4.5-mile length terminating at a warm inn. The trail is like a park—well groomed and civilized. The Ellis River Trail has one-way sections, offering north and south corridors. Each direction yields a different experience.

The Hall Trail runs nearly 7.5 miles and offers both a challenge and vistas of Mount Isolation and Wildcat Mountain as it crests Popple Mountain. Though the climb is long, so is the winding and exhilarating downhill. The views of the eastern range of the Presidentials from clearcuts are worth the trip. Add a couple of connector trails to this exciting downhill and you have the makings of a day's outing.

The trails are part of the Jackson Ski Touring Foundation, a nonprofit membership organization formed in 1972 to maintain cross-country ski trails in and around beautiful Jackson village. The system uses the land of seventy-five private landowners and town municipal land and operates

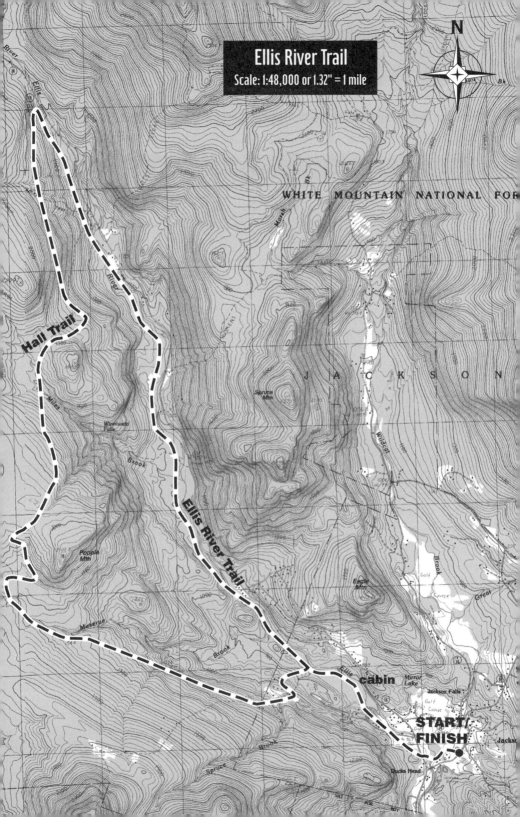

Gliding over a bridge, this cross-country skier crosses a rocky stream.

in the White Mountain National Forest through a special-use permit. The network of sixty-five trails covers 100 miles and has been host to a number of world-class events, including the 1990 World Nordic Disabled Championships, the 1985 International Relays, and the 1984 and 1995 NCAA College Championships.

From ski headquarters, ski west past the white-steepled church, across the flats of the open fields, and over a covered bridge. A tunnel provides access to the far side of Route 16 before the route crosses Green Hill Road and the trail along the Ellis River begins. A time-trial station allows skiers the opportunity to clock themselves. The trail has a few quick dips and hills, with wide bridge crossings. A warming hut comes about a mile from Green Hill Road.

Several loop options and short side trips make themselves available, like a ski to Winniweta Falls, Gray's Field, and the old Dollof Farm site. The signs are well placed, and it is no effort to follow them.

The Ellis River Trail leads to the High Water Trail, a more difficult trail that darts in and along the river bank for about a mile before reaching the Rocky Branch parking lot. It is here that the Hall Trail begins.

Prepare to climb. The long climb up the Hall to Popple Mountain passes by clear-cuts with views of 4,005-foot-high Mount Isolation looming in the distance. After cresting the summit there is a quick descent and hairpin turn just before the trail passes Maple Mountain Loop (a 2.0-mile side trail). The long, wondrous downhill continues past a scenic vista you can access by a short side trail. Be sure to take it to see the eastern slope mountains, including Black, Doublehead, Kearsarge, Sable, Chandler, Tin, Thorn, and others. Just before the trail rejoins the Ellis River Trail, there is a steep and fast drop, which passes through the scenic wildlife area, Gray's Field, before heading back to the flats of the village.

Directions at a glance

0.0   Leave the touring center on the Wentworth Trail, eventually crossing a covered bridge and using a tunnel under Route 16.

0.7   Take off the skis, cross Green Hill Road, and continue right on the Ellis River Trail.

5.2   Turn left on the High Water Trail.

6.2   Turn left on the Hall Trail.

13.7 Turn right on the Ellis River Trail.

15.0 Cross Green Hill Road, turn left on the Wentworth Trail, and follow it a half mile back to the touring center.

How to get there

The Jackson Ski Touring Foundation is located on Route 16A in the village of Jackson. Head north on Route 16 from the Glen intersection of Routes 16 and 302. Travel 2 miles and turn right on Route 16A, going over the red-covered bridge. The center is in the village on the left about 0.5 mile from the covered bridge. If traveling from the north, take Route 16 south from Gorham, New Hampshire, 20 miles through Pinkham Notch to Jackson.

Upper Saco River Loop

Bartlett, New Hampshire

Type of trail:	▬▬ ◄ 🌑
Distance:	4.7 miles
Terrain:	Flat, a couple of hills
Trail difficulty:	More difficult
Surface quality:	Groomed, single tracked
Food and facilities:	Rentals (cross-country and snowshoes), lessons, a wax room, and snacks—including hot soups—are available at the touring center. After the ski try the Bear Notch Deli in Bartlett, (603) 374–2445.
Phone numbers:	Bear Notch Ski Touring Center, (603) 374–2277.

Back in 1994 a couple of homegrown Bartlett brothers—Doug and John Garland—decided to start a cross-country ski area on the family property, which bordered the Saco River and White Mountain National Forest. During the first year the fledgling area took only donations. Now, the laidback, low-key network has grown to some 40 miles of ski trails, which allow snowshoers, too. About 3 miles of trails are dedicated to snowshoeing.

The small touring center is beyond rustic. It is shining backwoods scenic and simple. Walk into the woodsy center and maybe there will be bread baking in the corner. Check out the pool table that has denim pants legs as pockets. The beams in the center haven't had their bark removed.

It is the western network with trails meandering along the rocky-bottomed Saco River that is the attraction for many beginners and intermediates. Along the rolling waters the trails look straight up at Crawford Notch to the west and the slopes of the Attitash Bear Peak ski area to the east. The fourteenth highest peak in New Hampshire, 4,680-foot Mount Carrigain, provides a snow-capped backdrop against the clear, wild river.

The Saco isn't the only waterway playing a part in the show that is the Upper Saco River Loop. The Albany Brook flows down to a small waterfall by a screened-in summer cabin. Skiers and snowshoers cross a small bridge by the falls and can stop to admire the scenery.

For the most part the trails at the Bear Notch Ski Touring Center are not named but numbered and circled with a snowflake. The Upper Saco River Loop is largely agreeable to beginner skiers, but its sharp, spirited

Upper Saco River Loop
Scale: 1:24,000 or 2.64" = 1 mile

N

FOREST

Ledge

B A R T

Cave
Mth

1007

SACO

682

BM
748.2
RR Br. 753
WL 732

Sawyer
Rock

762?

80?

Bartlett

START/FINISH

Trailer
Park

McKiels
Pond

796

Albany

E M O U N T A I N

945 ft

Res

Louisville
Brook

O N A L   F O R E S T

hills might cause them to seek an alternate route to the flats of the Saco.

The loop is a collection of trails that wind and weave their way through the woods, flats, and hills of the network. The trail that parallels the Saco, number 16, also affords skiers and snowshoers the opportunity for two miniloops, keeping them within the sights of the clear, white-topped waters.

From the touring center trail 10 winds through the woods to a road crossing. Once on the other side, trail 11 enters left, and here the path rolls across two stream crossings, followed by a short, steep downhill. Trail 12 is a flat experience, crossing over the train tracks that follow the river. It is when rounding a corner on trail 16 that the Saco comes into view. The trail goes oh-so-close to the water's edge, sometimes giving the impression that you are skiing on a beach or peninsula. Trails 17 (look for beaver dams) and 13 are flat connectors, with trail 13 providing a turn just after crossing a railroad bridge. Though the loop continues through the maples with trails 20 and 21, those seeking more river frontage views should take trail 30 from trail 13 for a flat 1.5-mile ski to River Road, before turning back.

Directions at a glance

0.0   Leave the back of the touring center on trail 10.

0.3   Take off skis to cross road, then turn left on trail 11.

1.5   Turn left on trail 12.

1.7   Bear left on trail 16, which has two loops. Ski each one clockwise. After the second, return along trail 16 to first loop. Bear to the left on trail 16.

3.0   Turn left on trail 12.

3.2   Turn left on trail 17.

3.7   Turn left on trail 13. As an option bear left on trail 30 for a round-trip 3.0-mile ski to River Road and back.

4.0   Turn right on trail 21.

4.2   Bear right on trail 20.

4.3   Take off skis to cross road and continue straight on trail 2.

4.5   Turn right on trail 1 and follow it 0.2 mile back to the touring center.

Back across the road the loop's final leg is on trail 2 by the waterfall. It leads to trail 1 and a footbridge back to the touring center.

How to get there

From North Conway travel west on Route 302 through Bartlett about 12 miles.

Cardigan Loop

Alexandria, New Hampshire

Type of trail:	🔵 ▬
Also used by:	Winter hikers, backcountry skiers
Distance:	3.7 miles
Terrain:	Hilly
Trail difficulty:	More difficult for snowshoers, most difficult for skiers
Surface quality:	Ungroomed
Food and facilities:	Portable toilets outside the Appalachian Mountain Club's Cardigan Lodge are available to day users. Water bottles can be topped off as well. Pick food up in Bristol at the market or convenience stores. Afterward, try the Bristol House of Pizza on Route 3A.
Phone numbers:	Appalachian Mountain Club's Cardigan Lodge, (603) 744–8011, for trail information.

Mount Cardigan, or "Old Baldy," is one of those mountains special to followers of various activities. For the hiker the relatively easy ascent to the rocky dome affords excellent views along the open-faced slab ledges. Cardigan's 3,121-foot summit is a goal of many a beginner hiker.

For the backcountry skier Cardigan provides a sense of belonging and history. Before the modern ski lift transported skiers to the top of a mountain for a run down groomed corduroy boulevards, rugged Appalachian Mountain Club volunteers in the early 1930s had transformed a barn on the east side of Cardigan into what evolved into the Cardigan Lodge, built in 1939. They cut ski trails, the first being the 1.0-mile-long Duke's Run down the north peak of Cardigan, called Firescrew. Over the years the Civilian Conservation Corps stepped in to cut other trails, like the 0.75-mile Alexandria Ski Trail named after the neighboring small town.

Snowshoers and skiers now head to Cardigan to tackle the small network of trails mostly designed for the better backcountry skier. Novice skiers will find little choice, while strong intermediate skiers may find a challenge.

Directions at a glance

0.0 Leave the parking area on the Holt Trail.

1.1 Arrive at Grand Junction. Turn left on Cathedral Forest Trail.

1.7 Turn right on the Clark Trail.

1.9 Turn right on the Alexandria Ski Trail.

2.6 Bear right on the Holt Trail 1.1 miles back to the parking area.

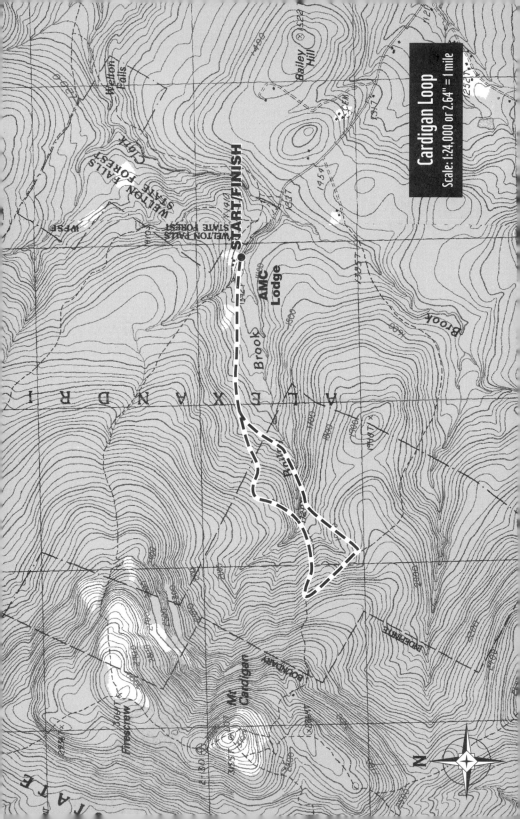

As snowshoeing gains in popularity, a trip up Cardigan could become a rite of passage as well. However the exposed ledges can be exposed to severe wind and become extremely icy. Your trip does not go to the summit though. Instead it combines several popular hiking trails, which lead to a stunning outcrop of views, including the cliffs of Firescrew and the swelling hills of southern New Hampshire. Though many skiers just ski up and then down the Alexandria Ski Trail, this loop affords the opportunity to combine a snowshoe and ski experience.

Starting at the lodge the Holt Trail is a wide, gravel road through the low hardwood forest. Travel past a snow-covered picnic area and pass a boundary into the Mount Cardigan State Park. Bailey Brook rushes by as the trail ascends gently to the Bailey Brook Bridge.

Cross the bridge and the trail ascends more moderately until it comes to an area of commingling

Skiers and snowshoers can choose from many options at the base of Mount Cardigan.

trails called Grand Junction. From here those on skis can pick up the Alexandria Ski Trail for the up-and-down experience. Snowshoers are not allowed on the ski trail.

By turning left on the yellow-blazed Cathedral Forest Trail, snowshoers will be traveling on the easiest eastern route up Cardigan—several switchbacks through a section of the forest damaged by the ice storm in January 1998.

The Cathedral Forest hands off to the Clark Trail through a grove of evergreens. You travel on more switchbacks until the trail joins up with the Alexandria Ski Trail near a spot called PJ Ledge. From this vantage point enjoy the views. Those seeking the summit experience can turn left and head up 0.7 mile on the Clark Trail, crossing exposed slab areas and passing two cabins.

For the most part the expert Alexandria Ski Trail is about 20 feet wide, but it is narrower at the onset. It is best tackled by expert backcountry skiers after about a foot of fresh powder. Expect steep drops (20 to 25 degrees) and twists as it winds its way back down to Grand Junction. Here you can cross the Bailey Brook Bridge again. The Holt Trail leads you back to the parking area.

How to get there

From I–93 take exit 23 and travel on Route 104 west to Bristol. In Bristol take Route 3A north about 2.5 miles. Turn left at the blinking light onto West Shore Road. In about 2.0 miles the road will bear to the right. Go straight. In about 1.0 mile a sign will point to the AMC. Take that right on Fawler River Road. Some 3.3 miles later another sign will point to the AMC. That's a left on Brook Road. Follow Brook Road and make a right on Shem Valley Road—where there is another AMC sign. Follow the road to the lodge and trailhead. Four-wheel drive is suggested for the final stretch on Shem Valley Road to the lodge.

Battery Seaman Loop

Odiorne Point State Park, Rye, New Hampshire

Type of trail:	
Also used by:	Walkers
Distance:	Nearly 2.0 miles
Terrain:	Flat
Trail difficulty:	Easiest
Surface quality:	Ungroomed, but skier tracked
Food and facilities:	Odiorne Point State Park and the Seacoast Science Center are adjacent to each other. Both charge small admission fees. No facilities are available in the park, but rest rooms and water are available at the center. There is a shopping center located at the junction of Routes 1 and 1A in Portsmouth for last minute lunch items. Yoken's Restaurant (603–436–8224) is a landmark seacoast restaurant.
Phone numbers:	New Hampshire Division of Parks and Recreation, (603) 271–3556; Seacoast Science Center, (603) 436–8043.

The crashing of waves against the rocky shore and the invigorating smell of the sea are not elements usually associated with snowshoeing and cross-country skiing. On a trip to Odiorne Point State Park in Rye, visitors not only get a taste of the sea, but nature and history as well. The park and Seacoast Science Center sit side by side. If the chill of winter is too cold, head inside to the exhibits to learn about Odiorne's role in United States history, the placement of fortifications around the point in World War II, or the nature of tidepools. Perhaps your visit will coincide with a lecture, children's story hour, or scavenger hunt.

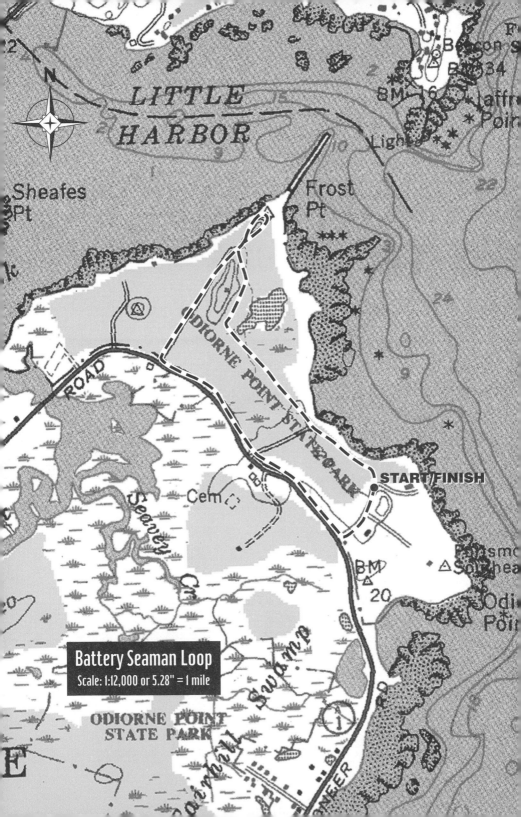

LITTLE
HARBOR

Sheafes
Pt

Frost
Pt

Light

Beacon S

BM 34

BM 16

Jaffrey
Point

ROAD

DIORNE POINT STATE PARK

Cem

Seavey

START/FINISH

BM
20

Portsmouth
Southea

Odiorne
Point

Odiorne Point
State Park

Campbell Swamp

PIONEER

Battery Seaman Loop
Scale: 1:12,000 or 5.28" = 1 mile

E

Be forewarned about snow conditions on the seacoast. A thaw can melt the snow quickly. It's not unusual for visitors to end up walking instead of heading out on skis.

Odiorne Point, on 300 acres of coastline, was made a state park in 1961. Here is where fishermen from Scotland landed in 1623 to establish one of the first European settlements in the country. When World War II began, Fort Dearborn was built at the point to protect Portsmouth Harbor from possible attack. The batteries remain where the military pointed their huge guns toward the sea.

The trail network in the park is not well signed. But there are plenty of landmarks and interpretive panels that make doing this loop an easy task.

The loop begins just around to the right by Battery 204, where massive shells are left out for display next to picnic tables. You'll see the battery when driving into the park. Park your car to the right. Then head over behind the tollbooth and follow the road with the sign that says BUS PARKING.

The trail begins to the left by a few large rocks and wooden trees. Head in through the thicket of trees. The trail takes a left. Look out on the waters where snow meets the sea. The trail hugs the shoreline and offers many views of the lighthouse in the distance. A couple of trails enter from the right. Ignore them. The trail swings to the left away from the shore. It's nice and wide.

At about 0.5 mile bear right through a grove of trees. There is a marsh through the trees on the right. Soon, you pass the Battery Seaman. Head in and explore. But it's just graffiti. The trail heads to the right as you pass a second part of the battery. At the far side of the battery, look out at the boats and docks. A trail to Frost Point enters right. Take it and loop around. At the point interpretive signs detail the history of and add a bit of insight into the life of a beach inhabitant—the sandworm. The sandworm, usually found along the coast in mud or sand, is generally used as fishing bait. The lighthouse is out in the distance, and a spit heads out into the water.

Directions at a glance

0.0 Leave the parking area through the posts and rocks.

0.5 Bear right by the fresh water marsh and soon see the Battery Seaman.

0.8 Bear right to Frost Point and follow the loop.

0.9 Continue straight and go past the other side of the Battery Seaman.

1.2 Turn left onto bike path by fence and gate.

1.7 Turn left by park entrance.

1.8 Turn right, back to parking lot.

Complete the loop and continue straight ahead to the other side of the battery, built in 1942. Shoot straight down through the wide, flat trail. Pass the battery and then keep an eye out for a World War II structure on the left. (It is filled with graffiti and not worth stopping for).

The trail then interesects a bike path by a fence and gate. Turn left. The path parallels Route 1A. It will pass a fresh water pond on the left, where you'll find more interpretive signs. The straight shot continues to the park entrance. Here a left takes you back to the first battery and the parking lot.

How to get there

From the Portsmouth Traffic Circle, exit via Route 1 Bypass south to Route 1. Turn left at the lights with Elwyn Road (sign points to Route 1A). At Foyes Corner go straight through at the stop sign to Route 1A. Follow Route 1A to Odiorne State Park Fort Dearborn site and turn left.

Heald Pond Trail

Wilton, New Hampshire

Type of trail:	
Also used by:	Hikers
Distance:	2.0 miles
Terrain:	Flat
Trail difficulty:	Easiest
Surface quality:	Ungroomed, skier tracked
Food and facilities:	No facilities here, so bring all you need to eat and drink. After the jaunt try the Peterborough Diner (603–924–6202) on Depot Street.
Phone numbers:	Society for the Protection of New Hampshire Forests, (603) 224–9945; for emergencies, 911.

Heald Pond is a delight to explore in winter. It is an easy snowshoe or ski through red maple, white pine, and hemlock. The pond itself offers fine views of Fisk Hill. Its twenty-five numbered identification stations along the way make the 2-mile trek go faster. The Pond Loop is very well marked with yellow blazes. The trail goes near the pond's edge, an apple orchard, beaver lodge, and stone wall.

The sixty-nine-acre pond is part of the Heald Tract, a preserve of the Society for the Protection of New Hampshire Forests. The land was

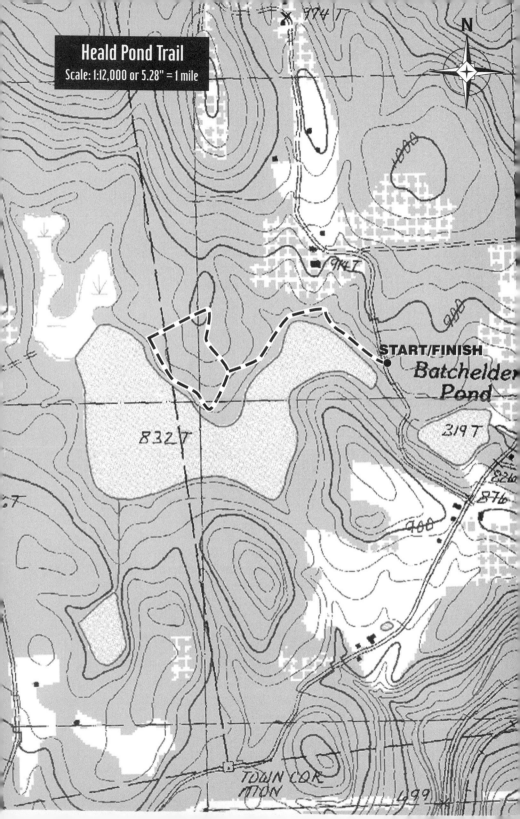

A horse takes hay from a snowshoer.

Directions at a glance

0.0 Follow the Pond Trail.

0.6 The Ledge Trail enters from the right, but continue straight on the Pond Trail.

0.7 The Look-See Trail enters left. Turn right and continue on the Pond Trail.

1.0 The Ledge, Spring, and Fisk Hill Trails enter. Turn right on the Pond Trail.

1.2 Turn right on the Ledge Cut-off Trail.

1.5 Turn left on the Pond Trail.

1.9 Cross the road back to the parking area.

donated in 1986 and has grown to encompass 500 acres with about 6 miles of walking and hiking paths. The property straddles Wilton and Temple and is such an excellent spot for introducing children to the natural world that the fourth graders of Wilton Elementary School in 1987–88 wrote a small guide to go along with the numbered stations (offered by the Society for the Protection of New Hampshire Forests). The trek is not diminished without the guide. But here we'll try and give some information that the children have shared.

The Pond Loop is directly across the parking area and is marked with a yellow blaze. The trail continues to the pond and bears right over a drainage into the woods. Here you'll see the first of the markers. Journey along the stations on the flat trail. The first ten identify red maple, white pine, mountain laurel, partridge berry, hemlock, elm, witch hazel, red oak, a den tree, and the decay of a log.

Pass the stone wall built from rocks left from glaciers and bear left into an open field that then reenters the woods. Just after station 14, which details fungus on a birch tree, travel over a narrow footbridge and enjoy the walk along the shore. There is a beaver lodge to see. Continue along the pond's edge and look for the orchards and an abandoned farm. Head back into the woods and cross another narrow footbridge. The Look-See Trail soon enters from the left. It's a short walk to the shores of the pond for a look and see. Continue left on the Pond Trail. Soon you'll have a stone wall to follow and stepping stones to help you through a wet area.

The blue-blazed Fisk Hill Trail enters after station 25.

Stay on the Pond Trail. The path widens and climbs for just a short spell. It is very quiet here. The Pond Trail gives way to the right. Choose the Ledge Cut-off. The climb continues a bit more but then descends and winds past huge, flat rock ledges.

The trail comes out at a junction with the Pond Trail. Turn left on the Pond Trail. If those snowshoe imprints or ski tracks look familiar, they could be yours. You have been here before.

Retrace your steps along the Pond Trail and enjoy the solitude.

How to get there

From Peterborough or points west, take Route 101 east to Route 31 south in Wilton and turn right. From the Nashua area take Route 101 west to Route 31 south in Wilton and turn left. Travel 2.5 miles and turn right on King Brook Road. At 0.9 mile turn left on Kimball Hill Road. It's a short 0.1 mile to a right on Heald Road. Follow the road 0.3 mile and park at the second plowed area after the HEALD TRACT SOCIETY FOR THE PROTECTION OF NEW HAMPSHIRE FORESTS sign on the right. The Pond Trail leaves from the parking area across the road. Parking is limited to a couple of vehicles.

Bear Brook State Park Loop

Allenstown, New Hampshire

Type of trail:	━━━ ⬤
Also used by:	Hikers, portions by snowmobilers, dogsledders
Distance:	5.0 miles
Terrain:	Flat to rolling
Trail difficulty:	Easiest
Surface quality:	Ungroomed, single tracked, double tracked
Food and facilities:	Primitive toilets are located at the trailhead parking area and at a few places along the loop. There is a shelter just off the loop that makes a fine stop for lunch overlooking Smith Pond. No camping is allowed. No water is available during the loop. As for food the best bet is at the junction of Routes 3 and 28 in Allenstown. There is a grocery store and a restaurant, Chantilly's.
Phone numbers:	For an emergency, 911; for information on Bear Brook State Park, call the New Hampshire Division of Parks and Recreations, Trails Bureau, (603) 271–3254.

The beauty of Bear Brook State Park is that there is something for everyone. With nearly 10,000 acres of forest, there is room for the snowshoer, cross-country skier, snowmobiler, and even the dogsledder. At times they may cross each other's path, but for the most part the networks are separate.

The loop through Bear Brook utilizes several different trails—Little Bear, Bobcat, Broken Boulder, and Pitch Pine. Tie them all together and you have quite an enjoyable bundle. Birch, pine, red oak, and hemlock trees make up much of the forest you'll be passing through. There are also a few clearings, areas of downed trees off the trails, and "snags," dead standing trees left for wildlife to use. For example, woodpeckers eat the insects found in these trees. Commercial timber sales have taken place in the park, and signs up near the beginning of the loop explain what has taken place in the area. You'll spot (deer scat) and hear (fluttering of a game bird taking off) evidence of wildlife. Trail conditions can vary tremendously with the amount of snowfall and season.

A rustic shelter that overlooks the marshy Smith Pond is a good place to rest and have a bite to eat. It's not too many trails that cross through an archery range, and this loop does, skirting Archery Pond and the targets used by archers in the nonsnow months when the range is open.

Circular blue signs bearing the letters *XC* mark the trails. Blue arrows point the way, too. Every once in a while you'll pass a number that is just

an indicator of where you are according to the state maps available at the trailhead.

Leave the parking lot on the Little Bear Trail, zip down, and turn left at the sign for the Little Bear Trail. The trail is wide and rises gently. New growth pine, tree stumps, and snags are evidence of a December 1996 logging operation. Posted signs explain what happened.

Little Bear Trail bears to the left and starts climbing along a hill. The trail narrows and winds upward. There is a bit of relief with a few rolling sections. Snake around a big sand pit and enjoy the ride before coming to a green gate where the trail crosses a snowmobile path (Hayes Farm Trail). Little Bear continues straight and gently slopes downward. Pass some toilets and come out at a summer parking area. Stay to the left and look for the blue XC signs. Turn left by the sign that says XC 9 and points to the Chipmunk and Bobcat Trails. The path is the Bobcat Trail. Skirt the marsh. Tall evergreens appear to stand guard to welcome your arrival. The Bobcat is an easy grade. There will be several trail junctions that are easy to follow for the rest of the loop. Bobcat is a straight shot and wide for some time. Flat rocks line the road at times. Take notice of the leaves that have turned brown but have not yet fallen. Bobcat bears hard to the left before a long, rollicking down-

Directions at a glance

0.0 From parking area leave via the Little Bear Trail.

0.1 Turn left on Little Bear Trail. The Bear Brook Trail goes straight.

0.4 Bear left on the Little Bear Trail.

1.5 Stay straight on the Bobcat Trail by the XC 9 sign.

2.0 Stay straight on the Bobcat Trail at XC 14.

3.0 Turn left on the Broken Boulder Trail at XC 7.

3.5 Bear left on Broken Boulder at XC 6.

4.2 Turn right by the archery range at XC 3 on Pitch Pine Trail. Follow it 0.8 to the parking area.

hill. Turn left on the wide Broken Boulder Trail at the junction (XC 7). Soon the path to the Smith Pond Shelter leaves left. It's a good rest spot.

Stay on Broken Boulder as it winds down. Broken Boulder bears left at the junction with the Pitch Pine Trail and goes around the pond.

Cross over Podunk Road and stay straight on Broken Boulder. Continue the decent, cross a snowmobile trail, and enjoy the winding descent. You'll soon cross the only bridge.

A tunnel of small evergreens leads to signs of the archery range. At the clearing turn right and head down through the range on the edge of Archery Pond, by the targets, toilets, and picnic tables.

The trail undergoes a personality change after this—it becomes schizophrenic. It's a winding roller coaster and crosses various snowmobile paths and a gravel pit in an area of a November 1996 timber cut. But this lasts only a short while because the end of the loop is in sight. Broken Boulder now becomes the Pitch Pine Trail. Stay with it until the end. There are a couple of buildings up ahead. Near them, head back down to the parking area where the loop began.

How to get there

Take I–93 to exit 13. Travel on Route 3 south to Route 28 north in Allenstown. Turn left and travel about 3.0 miles to sign at entrance to Bear Brook State Park. This is the Allenstown-Deerfield Road. Turn right at the sign and travel 3.2 miles to Podunk Road. Turn right on Podunk Road and travel 0.3 mile to skier parking area on right.

Mount Monadnock Loop

Monadnock State Park, Jaffrey, New Hampshire

Type of trail:	⬭ , portions for ▬▬
Also used by:	Hikers
Distance:	4.6 miles
Terrain:	Flat to steep
Trail difficulty:	Most difficult, easiest portion for CC
Surface quality:	Ungroomed
Food and facilities:	Monadnock State Park is open year-round but is staffed only on weekends and holidays during winter. Winter camping and pit toilets are available. Bring your own water midweek. On weekends and holidays a ranger staffs the park store from 8:30 A.M. to 4:30 P.M. There visitors can get the latest snow conditions and trail information and stock up on last-minute food items. As of 1998 rangers collected a day-use service charge of $2.50 per adult. During the week there was no ranger collecting. Pets are prohibited year-round. For those visiting during the week, maps are available at the toll booth. For a late lunch try the Rusty Bucket Cafe (603–532–4101) on Main Street in Jaffrey.
Phone numbers:	Monadnock State Park manager, (603) 532–8862; New Hampshire State Police, (800) 525–5555; for medical emergencies, 911.

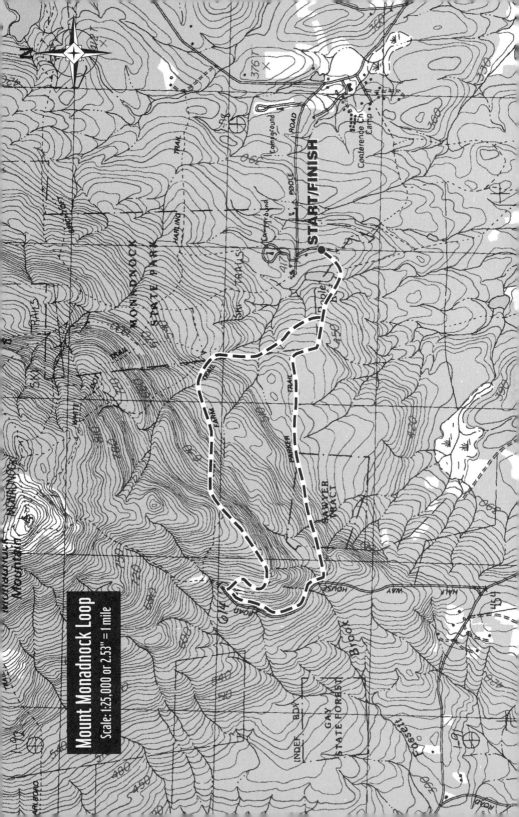

START/FINISH

Mount Monadnock Loop
Scale: 1:25,000 or 2.53" = 1 mile

Mount Monadnock is the crown jewel in southwestern New Hampshire's treasure—Monadnock State Park. At 3,165 feet Monadnock's rocky summit is arguably the most climbed mountain in the world. More than 40 miles of hiking trails surround it, and in winter some 14 miles of ungroomed cross-country skiing is available. Keep in mind that snowshoes do not belong on the treeless summit with inadequate snow cover.

The snowshoe loop suggested here is not up the mountain but on its southern flank, on trails once walked by Emerson and Thoreau. This loop is only for the most experienced snowshoers. Crampons are a must. Wooden snowshoes without crampons will not suffice.

The terrain moves quickly from flat to steep with the narrow Cliff Walk trail aptly named. From its heights the views extend south to Gap Mountain and southeast to Wachusett in Massachusetts, east to the Wapacks, and southwest to Mount Greylock. But in winter portions of Cliff Walk can become icy and in a couple of spots glissading would be helpful to navigate the rocky outcrops. Those unfamiliar with the mountain should wait a few days after a snowfall so that footprints in the snow can show the way to the upper reaches, especially between the Point Surprise and Hello Rock section of Cliff Walk. The elevation rises from about 1,300 feet to 2,300 feet.

As for the ski trails at the base of the mountain, they are primarily old logging roads, bridle paths, and summer hiking trails—all ungroomed. Six to ten inches of snow are needed for adequate skiing.

Directions at a glance

0.0 From the trailhead to the Parker Trail, head over the footbridge and along the trail.

0.6 Turn right on the Lost Farm Trail.

1.8 Head straight when you reach Cliff Walk.

2.1 Point Surprise Trail enters from the right. Stay left.

2.3 Turn right on Hello Rock Trail.

2.5 Turn left on Old Toll Road.

3.1 Turn left on Parker Trail and follow it 1.5 miles to the park headquarters.

The Parker Trail, on which the snowshoe loop begins, is a beginner ski trail. It can be snowshoed, too. Put skis on after crossing the footbridge and ascend the forested trail by the reservoir fence. Note the frozen drips of ice and the waterfall. The ski or snowshoe is 1.5 miles out to the Old Toll Road. Take it back for a 3.0-mile excursion. The trail is blazed in yellow. It is lined in part by portions of an old stone wall that once was part of a road to Keene. There are a few wet drainage areas to negotiate. At 0.6 mile the Lost Farm Trail enters from the right. Huge boulders soon come into view. The boulders were plucked from the south side of the mountain when a glacier moved through. The Cliff

Walk Trail enters from the right 0.5 mile later. It's another 0.4 mile to the Old Toll Road (a plowed road), which once led to a hotel that stood from 1860 to 1954. Return the same way, enjoying the descent.

The snowshoe loop begins at the Parker Trail trailhead, too. Follow it and link up to the Lost Farm Trail by turning right at 0.6 mile. The Lost Farm Trail ascends, sometimes steeply, near huge fallen boulders. The trail is blazed in white, while the stone wall follows a blue blaze. The forest changes to evergreens. Look out at the views of neighboring Massachusetts.

As the trail nears Cliff Walk, rocks and ice unite. Caution: Watch for icy stretches now. Follow the Cliff Walk to the left for awe-inspiring beauty. The edge of the trail plunges dramatically. Look for a sign out by the rocks that says AINSWORTH SEAT, named after Rev. Laban Ainsworth, the first settled minister of Jaffrey, who purchased 200 acres south of the summit in 1784.

After the Ainsworth Seat the trail enters the trees again and drops quickly through a pair a rocks, where glissading might be a good idea, to a junction with the Point Surprise Trail. There is a sign. Stay left on Cliff Walk for another shot at the ledges. The trail descends steeply again to a junction with the Hello Rock Trail. Two huge, beefy boulders mark the crossing. Turn right on the Hello Rock Trail and return to the trees. Soon a tunnel of pines provides a thoroughfare to a clearing.

The Cliff Walk Trail descends steeply to the left. It is not recommended as a snowshoe trail to those unfamiliar with the area.

Soon you'll spot a couple of buildings through the trees. This is by the Halfway House Site, where a hotel once stood. Now it is a private residence. Hello Rock is a pleasant jaunt downward. A clearing provides a bit of relief. The Hello Rock Trail continues to the left as the Thoreau and Point Surprise Trails enter from the right. Shortly enter the Halfway House Site clearing. Here one sign points to the White Arrow Trail, another to Hedgehog, Noble, Do Drop, and Side Foot Trails. Interestly enough turn left on the obvious Old Toll Road, which is not signed initially. Head down a few yards and pass a sign that points to the Old Halfway House Trail.

Respect the sign that says PRIVATE and continue down the plowed road for about 0.6 mile and then turn left on the yellow-blazed Parker Trail. The trail descends for most of its way back to the parking lot at the park headquarters.

How to get there
From Jaffrey travel on Route 124 west, through Jaffrey Center. Turn right on Dublin Road at 2.3 miles where a sign points to Monadnock State Park. Follow Dublin Road 1.4 miles to Poole Road, where you'll see

another sign for Monadnock. Turn left. You reach a plowed parking area by making a left after the tollbooth. This is parking lot number one. At the far end of the parking area is a plowed road that goes to a second parking area. Here parking is limited. The trailhead is reached by making a left at the fence surrounding Poole Reservoir. A sign marks the beginning of the trail.

Kilburn Loop

Pisgah State Park, Hinsdale, New Hampshire

Type of trail:	
Also used by:	Hikers
Distance:	6.4 miles
Terrain:	Flat to rolling
Trail difficulty:	Easiest to more difficult
Surface quality:	Ungroomed
Food and facilities:	There are no facilities on this excursion. Stock up on food in Hinsdale and Chesterfield, on opposite ends of Route 63. It is very important to bring plenty of food and fluids if you are planning to do the entire loop.
Phone numbers:	Pisgah State Park, (603) 239–8153; New Hampshire State Police, (800) 525–5555.

With more than 13,500 acres of forest, the twenty-one square miles of Pisgah State Park make it the largest property in the New Hampshire State Park system. The park is located in the southwestern corner of the state, not far from Brattleboro, Vermont, or the Massachusetts border. Seven ponds, four highland ridges, and several wetlands are all protected by the park, located between the small towns of Chesterfield and Hinsdale.

Miles of trails meander through the park. Some are part of the state's snowmobile corridor system, while others are open to multiple use, including the snowmobile. The six trailheads that lead into the park offer many options, but the Kilburn Loop is for human-powered vehicles only.

The Kilburn Loop itself is a 5.0-mile-long loop through evergreens, beech, hemlock, and occasional maple. You'll spot a trio of beaver ponds through the woods, and part of the trip skirts the western shores of the quiet Kilburn Pond. You can travel on it in either direction, but we prefer to save the level grades along the pond's shores for the end of the tour,

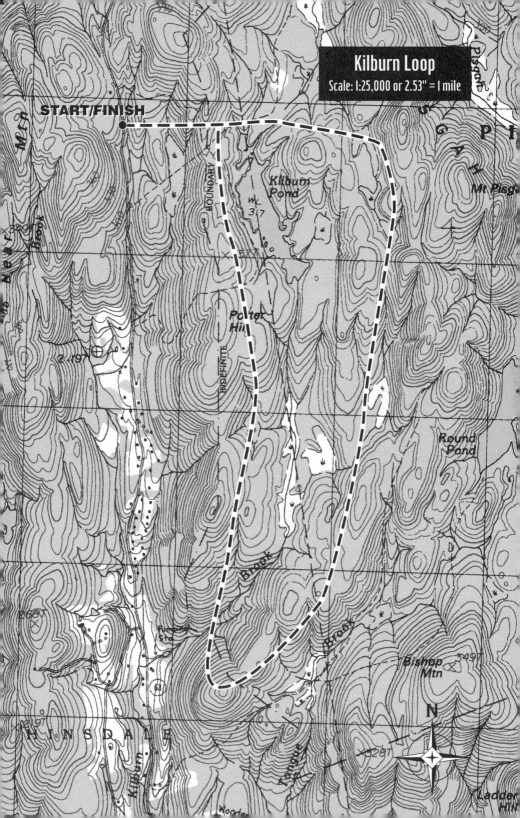

instead of the beginning. For those skiers and snowshoers looking for a shorter outing, this too can be had. Instead of taking the loop clockwise, as suggested here, take it just a mile or so counterclockwise, find a secluded spot along the rolling bank, have a bite, and head back.

Begin by leaving the well-marked trailhead. The trail, called Kilburn Road, is wide at this point and will soon dip down to the pond. Look for the work of the pileated woodpecker among the trees. It's not that hard to find.

The road heads down to a junction. Those just seeking a pondside picnic can head right and scoot back after dessert. The rest of us, turn left at the sign that reads KILBURN LOOP, and we will save views of the pond for later in the day.

This sheltered romp through the forest is blazed with blue diamonds. At about 0.1 mile from the junction, the trail turns to the right over a bridge with handrails. Notice the darkness once through the evergreens. Though winter, it's warm and cozy in here. The trail begins to ascend. Take a look around and notice the patterns of nature in the snow. Pine cones, pine needles, and other markers left by Mother Nature make the trail a gallery of natural spin art.

The trail rolls up and down, sometimes steeply. Up on the right, it climbs to a ridge from the forest floor. The Pisgah Mountain Trail enters from the left, but bear right and see the sign that says PISGAH LOOP 4.3. There are flat and narrow sections here, too. A yellow caution sign is your signal for a nice winding downhill.

> ## Directions at a glance
>
> 0.0 From the trailhead take Kilburn Road 0.7 mile.
>
> 0.7 Bear slightly left on Kilburn Loop.
>
> 0.8 Turn right and cross bridge.
>
> 1.4 Bear right as Pisgah Mountain Trail enters from the left.
>
> 5.7 Bear left back on Kilburn Road to trailhead.

The trail snakes to the left and heads though a bit of a boulder field, covered in snow, trees and their roots wrapped around the rocks. Head down and peer through the trees on the left to see a beaver pond. The trail heads up to the right again, sometimes steeply. Listen closely for the music of winter's songbirds.

Darkness gives way to light as the beech and hemlock hold court. The noon sun leads the way. Head down a gentle grade and snake around a ledge. Corn snow tops the crust as the sun beats down. The corn is a harbinger of playful months to come.

Up and down you go. When you come to a footbridge, the trail turns to the right. At the left is a beaver pond. The trail widens and heads up.

A snowshoer reads the signs at the entrance to Pisgah State Park and the start of the Kilburn Pond Loop.

Then down it goes again, a long, pleasant downhill. It then bears to the right. You cross a bridge and another long ascent begins. Cross one more bridge (look for the old bridge to the left) and continue on up.

You'll hear the rushing waters of Kilburn Brook. Slide down and come to a fourth bridge, a narrow span by yet a third beaver pond.

The roller coaster continues. High up on a ridge, then come down to gaze on the shore of Kilburn Pond. Follow its shores along the water's edge. Sometimes it can be marshy there. If you want, find your own way to the ice.

Stay with the trail and come to the sign that says KILBURN LOOP again. Bear left and climb for the last time. See the trailhead.

Rejoice!

How to get there

From I–91 in Vermont take exit 3 to 9 east in New Hampshire. Travel 6.0 miles. Make a right on Route 63 and travel about 4.5 miles south, through the village of Chesterfield. The Kilburn Road trailhead to Pisgah State Park is on the left. From Hinsdale take 63 north about 4.0. The trailhead is on the right.

Appendix

VERMONT SKI CENTERS

The following are cross-country skiing areas in Vermont:

Bolton Valley Touring Center
Bolton, VT 05477
Phone: (802) 434–2131

Burke Mountain Cross-Country
East Burke, VT 05832
Phone: (802) 626–8338

Catamount Family Center
Williston, VT 05363
Phone: (802) 879–6001

Craftsbury Nordic Ski Center
Craftsbury Common, VT 05826
Phone: (800) 729–7751

Edson Hill Manor
Stowe, VT 05672
Phone: (802) 253–8954

Hazen's Notch Cross-Counry
Montgomery Center, VT 05471
Phone: (802) 326–4708

Highland Lodge
Greensboro, VT 05841
Phone: (802) 533–2647

Jay Peak
Jay, VT 05859
Phone: (802) 988–2611

Smugglers' Notch Resort
Smugglers' Notch, VT 05464
Phone: (802) 644–8851

Sterling Ridge Inn
Jeffersonville, VT 05464
Phone: (802) 644–8265

Stowe Mountain Resort
Stowe, VT 05672
Phone: (802) 253–3000

Topnotch
Stowe, VT 05672
Phone: (802) 253–5719

Trapp Family Lodge
Stowe, VT 05672
Phone: (802) 253–5719

Blueberry Hill
Goshen, VT 05733
Phone: (802) 247–6735

Blueberry Lake Cross-Country
East Warren, VT 05674
Phone: (802) 496–6687

Churchill House Inn
Brandon, VT 05733
Phone: (802) 247–3078

Fox Run Ski Touring
Ludlow, VT 05149
Phone: (802) 228–8871

Green Mountain Touring Center
Randolph, VT 05060
Phone: (800) 424–5575

Green Trails Inn and Cross-
Country Center
Brookfield, VT 05036
Phone: (802) 276–3412

Mountain Meadows
Killington, VT 05751
Phone: (802) 775–7077

Mountain Top Cross-Country
Ski Resort
Chittenden, VT 05737
Phone: (802) 483–6089

Ole's
Warren, VT 05674
Phone: (802) 496–3430

Rikert's
Ripton, VT 05766
Phone: (802) 388–2759

Round Barn Farm
Waitsfield, VT 05673
Phone: (802) 496–2276

Sugarbush Resort
Warren, VT 05674
Phone: (802) 583–2605

Three Stallion Inn Cross-Country
Center
Randolph, VT 05060
Phone: (802) 728–5575

Wilderness Trails
Quechee, VT 05059
Phone: (802) 295–7620

Woodstock
Woodstock, VT 05091
Phone: (800) 448–7900

Brattleboro Outing Club
Brattleboro, VT 05301
Phone: (802) 254–4081

Grafton Ponds
Townsend Road
Grafton, VT 05146
Phone: (802) 843–2400

Hermitage Cross-Country Touring
Center
Wilmington, VT 05363
Phone: (802) 464–3511

The Landgrove Inn
Landgrove, VT 05148
Phone: (802) 824–6673

Meadow Brook Inn
Landgrove, VT 05148
Phone: (802) 824–6444

Merck Forest and Farmland Center
Rupert, VT 05768
Phone: (802) 394–7836

Prospect Mountain Cross-Country
Center
Woodford, VT
Phone: (802) 442–2575

Stratton Mountain Cross-Country
Stratton, VT 05155
Phone: (802) 297–4114

Tater Hill
Londonderry, VT 05148
Phone: (802) 824–6578

Timber Creek
Wilmington, VT 05363
Phone: (802) 464–0999

Viking Cross-Country
Londonderry, VT 05148
Phone: (802) 824–3933

Wild Wings
Peru, VT 05152
Phone: (802) 824–6793

White House
Wilmington, VT 05363
Phone: (802) 464–2135

NEW HAMPSHIRE SKI CENTERS

The following are cross-country skiing areas in New Hampshire:

The Balsams
Route 26
Dixville Notch, NH 03576
Phone: (800) 255–0600
E-mail: thebalsams@aol.com
Web site: www.thebalsams.com

Bear Notch Ski Touring Center
Route 302
Bartlett, NH 03812
Phone: (603) 374–2277
Web site: www.journeysnorth.com/
 Bearnotch

Bretton Woods
Route 302
Bretton Woods, NH 03575
Phone: (800) 232–2972
E-mail: skibw@brettonwoods.com
Web site: www.brettonwoods.com

Eastman Cross-Country Center
Grantham, NH 03753
Phone: (603) 863–4500

Franconia Village Cross-Country
1300 Easton Road
Franconia, NH 03580
Phone: (800) 473–5299
Web site: www.franconiainn.com

Great Glen Trails
Route 16
Pinkham Notch, NH 03581
Phone: (603) 466–2333
Web site: www.mt-washington.com

Gunstock
Route 11A
Gilford, NH 03246
Phone: (800) GUNSTOCK
Web site: www.gunstock.com

Jackson Ski Touring Foundation
Main Street
Jackson, NH 03846
Phone: (800) XC–SNOWS
E-mail: info@jacksonxc.com
Web site: www.jackson.com

King Pine
Route 153
East Madison, NH 03849
Phone: (800) FREE–SKI
E-mail: info@purityspring.com
Web site: www.purityspring.com

Loon Mountain
Route 112
Lincoln, NH 03251
Phone: (603) 745–8111
E-mail: info@loonmtn.com
Web site: www.loonmtn.com

Mount Washington Valley
    Ski Touring
Route 16
Intervale, NH 03845
Phone: (603) 356–9920

Waterville Valley
Town Square
Waterville Valley, NH 03215
Phone: (603) 236–4666
E-mail: info@waterville.com
Web site: www.waterville.com

Nordic Skier
Routes 28/109
Wolfeboro, NH 03894
Phone: (603) 569–3151

Norsk Cross-Country
Route 11
New London, NH 03257
Phone: (800) 426–6775
E-mail: info@skinorsk.com
Web site: www.skinorsk.com

Windblown
Routes 124/123
New Ipswich, NH 03071
Phone: (603) 878–2869

Woodbound Inn
62 Woodbound Road
Rindge, NH 03461
Phone: (800) 688–7770
Web site: www.nhweb.com/wood-
    bound/index.com

RESOURCES

The following are resource organizations for snowshoeing and cross-country skiing in Vermont and New Hampshire:

Catamount Trail Association
P.O. Box 1235
Burlington, VT 05402
Phone: (802) 864–5794
E-mail: sherary@aol.com

Green Mountain Club
Route 100, R.R. 1, Box 650
Waterbury Center, VT 05677
Phone: (802) 244–7037
E-mail: gmcds@sover.net

Green Mountain National Forest
Forest Supervisor's Office
231 North Main Street
Rutland, VT 05701
Phone: (802) 747–6700

Mountain Valley Trails Association
P.O. Box 464
Londonderry, VT 05148
Phone: (802) 824–4166

Vermont Department of Forests,
Parks and Recreation
103 South Main Street
Waterbury, VT 05676
Phone: (802) 244–8711

Vermont Association of Snow
Travelers
P.O. Box 839
Montpelier, VT 05602
Phone: (802) 223–4316

Vermont Department of Tourism
and Marketing
134 State Street
Montpelier, VT 05602
Phone: (802) 828–3237
Web site: www.travel-vermont.com

Ski Vermont
P.O. Box 368
Montpelier, VT 05601
Phone: (802) 223–2439
Web site: www.skivermont.com

Appalachian Mountain Club
5 Joy Street
Boston, MA 02108
Phone: (617) 523–0636
Web site: www.outdoors.org

New Hamphire Department of
Travel and Tourism Develop-
ment
P.O. Box 1856
Concord, NH 03302
Phone: (603) 271–2343
Web site: www.visitnh.gov

New Hampshire Division of Parks
and Recreation
P.O. Box 1856
Concord, NH 03302
Phone: (603) 271–3556

Ski New Hampshire
P.O. Box 10
North Woodstock, NH 03262
Phone: (800) 887–5464
E-mail: info@skinh.com
Web site: www.skinh.com

Squam Lakes Association
P.O. Box 204
Holderness, NH 03245
Phone: (603) 968–7336

White Mountain National Forest
Supervisor's Office
719 North Main Street
Laconia, NH 03246
Phone: (603) 528–8721

United States Snowshoe Associa-
tion
Corinth, NY 12822
Phone: (715) 373–5556

American Hiking Society
P.O. Box 20160
Washington, DC 20041-2160
Phone: (301) 565–6704

Cross-Country Ski Areas Association
259 Bolton Road
Winchester, NH 03470
Phone: (603) 239–4341

Bibliography

The following books are valuable resources:

Appalachian Mountain Club. *AMC White Mountain Guide* (26th ed.). Boston, 1999.

Gange, Jared. *Hiker's Guide to the Mountains of New Hampshire.* Huntington, Vermont: Huntington Graphics, 1997.

Gange, Jared. *Hiker's Guide to the Mountains of Vermont.* Huntington, Vermont: Huntington Graphics, 1997.

Goodman, David. *Backcountry Skiing and Snowboarding Adventures: Classic Backcountry Tours in Maine & New Hampshire.* Boston: Appalachian Mountain Club, 1999.

Green Mountain Club. *Day Hiker's Guide to Vermont* (3rd ed.). Waterbury Center, Vermont, 1987.

Green Mountain Club. *Long Trail Guide* (24th ed.). Waterbury Center, Vermont, 1996.

Mudge, John. *The White Mountains: Names, Places and Legends.* Etna, New Hampshire: The Durand Press, 1992.

Preston, Philip. *The Squam Trail Guide.* Holderness, New Hampshire: Squam Lake Association, 1991.

Smith, Steve D. *Ponds and Lakes in the White Mountains.* Woodstock, Vermont: Backcountry, 1990.

Tilton, Buck, and Hubbell, Frank. *Medicine for the Backcountry.* (2nd ed.) Old Saybrook, Connecticut: The Globe Pequot Press, 1994.

About the Author

Marty Basch is an award-winning writer who has trouble sitting still. His bicycle has been a means for adventure and has led to books such as *Against the Wind* (which chronicles a Maine to Alaska bicycle odyssey), *Above the Circle* (Artic Scandinavia on a bicycle), and *The White Mountain Ride Guide*. He got off his wheels and onto his skis and snowshoes for *Winter Trails*. His articles have appeared in publications such as *Snow Country, SKI,* and *The Boston Globe*. He lives in the White Mountains of New Hampshire.